Unlocking the Triathlon

To my future triathlete, Oliver, and his dog, Daisy

Hilary JM Topper

Foreword by Julie Moss

UNLOCKING THE TRIATHLON

The Beginner's Guide to Competing in a Triathlon

Meyer & Meyer Sport

British Library Cataloguing in Publication Data
A catalogue record for this book is available from the British Library

Unlocking the Triathlon
Maidenhead: Meyer & Meyer Sport (UK) Ltd., 2026
ISBN: 978-1-78255-286-4

Aachen, Auckland, Beirut, Cairo, Cape Town, Dubai, Hägendorf, Hong Kong, Indianapolis, Maidenhead, Manila, New Delhi, Singapore, Sydney, Tehran, Vienna

Member of the World Sport Publishers' Association (WSPA), www.w-s-p-a.org

Printed by Versa Press, East Peoria, IL
www.versapress.com
Printed in the United States of America

ISBN 978-1-78255-286-4
Email: info@m-m-sports.com
www.thesportspublisher.com

Manufacturer under the GPSR
Meyer & Meyer Fachverlag und Buchhandel GmbH
Von-Coels-Str. 390
52080 Aachen, Germany
www.dersportverlag.de

CONTENTS

FOREWORD

Hilary and I met when she graciously invited me to appear on her podcast, *Hilary Topper On Air.* I talked about my book, *Crawl of Fame*, detailing my 1982 Ironman journey. Hilary also reviewed my book on her popular triathlon blog, *ATriathletesDiary.com*.

After that, we chatted and compared our endurance sports histories. We found many parallel moments, instantly bonding over our love for endurance sports and how they have positively impacted our lives.

Hilary and I discovered that during the most challenging moments of our respective endurance competitions, we overcame mental barriers and maintained a positive mindset by constantly reminding ourselves of our goals and why we were willing to push our limits.

We focused on the feeling of accomplishment and pride we would experience at the finish line, and this kept us motivated, even when we were exhausted and facing physical and mental challenges.

I eagerly cheer for Hilary as she publishes her fourth book, *Unlocking the Triathlon*. In this book, she offers anyone and everyone the opportunity to set and reach an endurance goal in triathlon.

As I delved into the pages of this empowering guide, tailored for anyone venturing into triathlons, I was reminded of the extraordinary potential within each of us.

Hilary's dedication to providing a comprehensive resource that caters to individuals' unique needs and challenges in these sports is truly commendable.

UNLOCKING THE TRIATHLON

In a world where limits are constantly tested, and boundaries are redefined, this book is a beacon of encouragement and support for every aspiring triathlete.

The journey from novice to seasoned athlete is both exhilarating and daunting, but with the right tools and guidance, barriers dissolve, and dreams transform into reality. These pages contain a wealth of knowledge, practical tips, and insightful advice that will empower you to conquer your doubts, push beyond your perceived limitations, and tap into the unwavering strength that resides within you.

Whether you are dipping your toes into the waters of triathlon for the first time or aiming to enhance your skills and performance, this book serves as a steadfast companion on your path to success.

To anyone who dares to dream, embraces challenges as opportunities, and embodies the spirit of resilience and perseverance, this book is a testament to your unwavering courage and determination.

It will ignite a fire within you, inspiring you to chase your goals with unwavering passion and resolve. As you embark on this transformative journey, remember that every stroke, pedal, and step brings you closer to your greatness.

Believe in your strength, trust in your abilities, and embrace the triathlete within. Here's to the remarkable journey that lies ahead. Dive in, pedal strong, run free, and may your spirit soar with every finish line you cross.

Hilary understands that triathlons have benefits that reach deep into the core of who we are. They build self-confidence through improved physical strength and mental toughness, challenge gender stereotypes, foster a sense of accomplishment, promote body positivity, teach resilience and perseverance, and offer relief from stress and anxiety.

Hilary's *Unlocking the Triathlon* encourages everyone to pursue their goals.

–Julie Moss
Ironman Hall of Fame Triathlete, speaker, and author of *Crawl of Fame*

PREFACE

Before I became a triathlete in May 2014, I didn't know where to start. I had many questions, so I sought out a coach who helped me navigate the process. I also looked for books on the subject, but I needed more. Most books I found were dedicated to elite or experienced athletes, and I didn't fit the bill. The ones I found for beginners were way too technical. That is why I decided to write this book.

Unlocking the Triathlon is a book written in simple language that will help you pass your first or fifteenth triathlon with flying colors.

Let me tell you a little about myself. For starters, I was never an athlete, and I didn't participate in sports in school, However, as I got older, I gained a lot of weight and had a poor body image. In addition, I had my own business and always felt stressed out. I needed to change.

I joined a gym for the first time and hired a trainer. He told me to warm up on the treadmill. Little did he know, I had never been on a treadmill before, so I didn't know how to turn it on. Luckily, the woman running next to me stopped what she was doing and showed me how it worked.

After that, I started running a little on the treadmill, then took it outside. Thankfully, I met a friend who enjoyed running, and we became running partners. We would run/walk every Sunday and enjoy each other's company. After a while, we decided to take "run-cations" together, and a couple of years later, we decided to compete in a triathlon.

After competing, I became addicted. I wanted to know everything I could about triathlons. I read books and blogs and tried to learn as much as possible from other triathletes.

Preface

In 2016, as a public relations practitioner with an event planning background, I combined my event-planning skills with my thirst for triathlon knowledge to organize the NY Tri Expo at Citi Field. The expo featured 20 concurrent seminars, 70 vendors, and 2,000 attendees. It was a fantastic event, and all the athletes who attended felt they learned a lot and were grateful.

That same year, I was accepted into the New York City Marathon. I asked Jeff Galloway, the former Olympian turned running coach best known his Run Walk Run method, to train me. The following year, I got certified with Jeff and started a run-walk group on Long Island. A few years later, I decided to get certified with the Road Runners Club of America (RRCA). Now, I am also a Level 1 RRCA running coach.

In 2019, I received my triathlon coaching certification. My blog, *ATriathletesDiary.com*, was successful, and in it, I wrote about training, new products, and more. But I felt I needed to have that expertise under my belt.

I attended a two-day in-person class in Clermont, Florida, and studied with USA Triathlon. Following that, I took a terrifying 100-question quiz and passed.

A couple of years after that, I went to Boston and signed up for the US Masters Swimming (USMS) program to get certified there. I spent two full days in Boston and became a Level 3 USMS Swim Coach plus an Adult Learn to Swim Coach.

After having knee surgery and recuperating in 2024, I took the WOWSA (World Open Water Swimming Association) course and became certified as an open-water swim instructor.

Because of my love for triathlons, I wrote my first endurance book, *From Couch Potato to Endurance Athlete: A Portrait of a Non-Athletic Triathlete*. It discussed my journey from non-athlete to endurance athlete. The book is a memoir but also a self-help book. My hope for writing was to get people to go outside their comfort zones and do something they never thought they could do, as I did.

Although I have accomplished much in the endurance space, I had to overcome many obstacles to do so. To me, triathlons are synonymous with life. You achieve incredible highs, but you also experience lows. When you finally cross that finish line, you feel a sense of accomplishment you have never known. And, when you come in slower than anticipated or don't finish a race, you can return stronger.

Triathlon is more than a sport; it's a testament to human endurance, resilience, and the relentless pursuit of personal excellence.

Unlocking the Triathlon was written for you, the aspiring triathlete. By reading it, you will learn all the basics, which will help you on your way to racing in many different triathlons across the country.

My door is always open, and if you have any comments or thoughts, please send them to me at hilarytopper@gmail.com.

Happy training!

ACKNOWLEDGMENTS

I want to acknowledge so many people. I am grateful to my publisher, Liz Evans of Meyer & Meyer Sport, for believing in me and my story. I would also like to thank Tom Doherty of Cardinal Press. Liz and Tom have been a pleasure to work with, and I appreciate them both.

My deepest gratitude goes to my training partner, Ray, and my entire run/walk team. You all are rock stars, and I genuinely appreciate you. I couldn't get through those long runs, bikes, and swims without you. The laughs and camaraderie are amazing.

I am grateful for my coaching clients. Helping you get to the next level helps me.

Recently, I started a USMS Master Swim Team. Teaching swimming lets me break down the stroke and focus on what's important.

I would like to extend a special thank you to my WeREndurance triathlon team. You are all incredibly supportive, and I appreciate each of you. I also want to thank my Strava and social media friends for always inspiring me to push forward.

Thanks to my husband, Brian, and children, Zoey, Dan, Derek, Daisy, and my new grandson, Ollie, for your ongoing love and support.

A special mention goes to my son, Derek, for providing outstanding editing suggestions, my sister-in-law, Andrea, who helped me proofread, and my friend and colleague, Lisa, for reading and re-reading various versions of this book.

Finally, thank you for taking the leap into triathlon training and reading this book.

INTRODUCTION

I competed in my first triathlon at the age of 53. Although I was a latecomer, I quickly developed a passion for the sport. Endurance sports provide a distinct perspective on self-discovery, allowing you to uncover your strengths and weaknesses.

My introduction to triathlons was somewhat unconventional. My involvement as a Google Glass Explorer facilitated it. For those unfamiliar with the term, Google Glass is a wearable technology headset that integrates augmented reality. It allows users to capture photos or videos instantly, share them on social media, ask questions, and even translate languages in real-time. While Facebook and Apple have since released similar products, they have yet to replicate the unique experience Google Glass offered. In 2011, I was invited to be part of the program and was an early adopter of wearable technology.

During an "exploration trip" to Sanibel, Florida, I wore my Google Glass and was approached by the Fort Myers/Sanibel tourism director. She informed me of a local event called the Captiva Triathlon. Intrigued by her description of the race and the prospect of testing my endurance, I decided to participate. Little did I know then how profoundly this decision would impact my life, igniting a love for endurance sports that continues to shape my identity and direction.

Before this experience, I had never participated in a triathlon or watched one on television. I had recently started to run, but agreeing to do a triathlon was stepping into uncharted territory, blissfully unaware of the challenges ahead.

This adventure began when my friend and I participated in the New York Road Runners' Brooklyn Half Marathon 2014. Around the 10th mile, my friend told me, "I will never do this again." She was tired and cranky, and her back hurt. While her statement disappointed me, as I felt energized and strong,

Finishing St. Anthony Triathlon in St. Petersburg, Florida.

it also presented an opportunity. I suggested we try something different: the Captiva Triathlon in Sanibel, remembering the tourism director's description.

And so began my journey into the world of triathlon. The nerves and anxiety that accompanied the race's preparation, participation, and aftermath might have led many to assume I'd had enough. Yet, contrary to expectations, I found myself captivated by the experience. Far from being deterred, I yearned for more opportunities to test my limits and immerse myself in this exhilarating sport.

Despite the considerable expense of my first triathlon—purchasing a new road bike, a wetsuit, and all the necessary gear—I discovered a passion worth every penny.

Over the years, this passion has propelled me through countless races nationwide. My love for triathlon grew so deep that I became a certified USA Triathlon (USAT) Coach, a USMS Swim Coach, an RRCA Running Coach, and a WOWSA Open-Water Swim Coach.

In 2022, I penned my first endurance book, *From Couch Potato to Endurance Athlete: A Portrait of a Non-Athletic Triathlete.* It chronicles my decade-long journey from taking my first run to competing in numerous triathlons nationwide.

While that book served as a memoir/self-help book, this one is designed to guide you through the triathlon world in straightforward and engaging language.

Moreover, I wanted to share stories of first-time experiences to inspire and motivate you. Throughout this book, I've included personal anecdotes from various triathletes, from pros to everyday athletes. I know these stories will inspire you to continue with your journey.

I also included some funny anecdotes from Facebook's Pathetic Triathlete group and my triathlon team, WeREndurance. I know you will get a chuckle out of these, but they are also there to teach you what to do or not to do in certain situations.

I hope you find this book enjoyable and informative, and that it ignites you with the same passion I have for triathlons.

Here's to joyful training! And remember to find your happy place!

PART 1
GETTING STARTED

Triathlons changed how I look at my career, family, and life. I am grateful that I found such an amazing sport that inspires and motivates me daily. –Hilary Topper, Author

CHAPTER 1

Why Become a Triathlete?

"I wanted to do a triathlon because I didn't want to train for a marathon."
–Pathetic Triathlete Member

What Is Your "Why?"

A "why" is a guiding light, providing purpose and direction. It's the reason that gets you out of bed for an early morning training session and pushes you to swim one more lap, bike one more mile, and run one more kilometer, even when every muscle in your body is begging you to stop.

With a why, the journey can seem manageable, and the goals can be attainable. The rigors of triathlon training—early mornings, strict diets, intense workouts, repeated cycles of exertion, and recovery—can become overwhelming without a motivating force driving the effort. The why frames these challenges as stepping stones toward a greater goal rather than insurmountable obstacles.

I became a triathlete because my running partner no longer wanted to run half marathons, so I suggested a triathlon. Looking back, this probably wasn't the most profound reason. However, in time, I realized that I began training for triathlons to prove to everyone, including myself, that I could do something challenging and outside my comfort zone.

Why do you want to compete in a triathlon? What will happen if you don't?

The why is personal and varies from person to person. For some, it's the allure of pushing their limits, of testing just how far their body and mind can go. Swimming, biking, and running over long distances offer an indescribable thrill, challenging every fiber of your being as you transcend the boundaries of what you believed was possible.

For others, it's about personal transformation. Perhaps they were on an unhealthy path and sought a drastic change, or they needed a way to cope with life's stresses. Triathlon offers a structured way to improve physical health and foster mental strength and discipline.

Many are drawn to the camaraderie and community within the world of triathlon. It's a sport that brings people together. It unites passion and respect for the demands of the three disciplines. Amid the sweat and the struggle, lifelong friendships are often forged.

Whether it's to try out something new and different or stand on the podium, the competitive nature of triathlons can be an irresistible draw. Then there's the allure of competition—the thrill of the race, the surge of adrenaline at the start line, and the satisfaction of crossing the finish line. It is intoxicating and emotional at the same time. My first coach said, "Trying to get on the podium gets me coming back."

Becoming a triathlete often serves a symbolic purpose. It proves you can balance multiple responsibilities and juggle tasks while still coming out on top, like handling the swim, bike, and run in a single event.

However, perhaps the most compelling reason is the sense of achievement from completing a triathlon. There's unique gratification in looking back on the grueling journey and knowing you completed it. It's an affirmation of strength, willpower, and tenacity that resonates far beyond the race.

The motivation behind becoming a triathlete often extends beyond the sport. It becomes a driving force that fuels consistency in training and pursuing other events and activities. The discipline, commitment, and resilience developed through triathlon training can also permeate other areas of life. For example, it has helped me in many ways, including organizational skills, juggling responsibilities, and staying consistent.

Triathletes may find themselves setting higher standards in their professional lives, pursuing personal goals with renewed vigor, or embracing other challenging hobbies. Many are business owners or overachievers in whatever

What Is a Pro Card?

In the triathlon, a pro card is like a special pass recognizing an athlete as a professional. Imagine if playing a sport was not only for fun but could also be your job, where you compete at the highest levels, possibly travel around, and even earn money from your races. A pro card separates the hobbyists from the pros.

To earn this card, athletes must prove they are among the best. This might mean finishing races quickly, beating many competitors, or achieving high competition scores.

Once you have a pro card, you can compete in unique races reserved for professionals. It could also lead to sponsorships, where companies give you products or money to support your training and racing.

they do. Triathlon can quickly become a passion for these folks—and it could become a passion for you, too!

What happens if you don't have a why? If you don't have a why or a solid reason for wanting to participate in a triathlon, this may be challenging, especially when faced with obstacles or setbacks.

It's important to note that not having a why isn't necessarily a permanent state. Often, people begin their triathlon journey without a clear reason, only to discover it along the way. The experience of training, the camaraderie among athletes, the thrill of competition, and the physical and mental transformation can spark a more profound purpose that fuels their triathlon journey. Discovering your why can be valuable, offering insights into personal strengths, passions, and values. Everyone's why is different. Dig deep and think about it. Once you do, you will be ready to sign up for your first triathlon.

QUICK TIP

- What's your why right now? Write it down and hang it in a prominent place so you can see it daily. It will help motivate and inspire you, especially on those cold, dreary days when you don't want to get out of bed.

Gwen Jorgensen
Triathlon Gold Medalist, Rio 2016 Olympics, Louisville, CO

Growing up, one of my cherished moments with my family involved biking to get ice cream. I was athletic in school, excelling as a seasoned swimmer and runner. However, my triathlon journey started in 2004 when my best friend, Maggie Lach, and I worked on a high school senior project. The project included doing a triathlon.

As a team, we decided to tackle a triathlon race in Pewaukee, Wisconsin. We would swim, bike, and run side by side. I used my mom's mountain bike since I didn't have a bike for this race.

Despite winning first and second places at the race, Maggie and I weren't driven by competitiveness but by the sheer joy of participating. After this event, triathlon slipped from my mind until 2010.

In college, I was a Division 1 swimmer and runner. USAT spotted my potential, citing my swimming and running background and assuring me that "anyone can ride a bike." They believed I had what it took to be a great triathlete.

With their support, I got a coach and a bike, and I was set to race in Clermont, Florida, to earn my pro card. (See sidebar for an explanation of a pro card.) This race was unique because obtaining a pro card typically requires participation in more than one race. However, this was the only race you needed to become a professional triathlete.

The transitions were lightning-fast during the race, and the competition was fierce, especially in the swim, where I was not used to people swimming over me.

It shocked my system and challenged me in unexpected ways, particularly mentally. Later, I learned to claim my space in the water, a significant shift from my initial strategy of letting others pass me by.

USAT's college recruitment program had previously introduced me to transitions through a camp, but experiencing them in a race environment was a different beast altogether. Wearing a wetsuit, for instance, highlighted different muscle soreness and emphasized the importance of choosing the right gear that doesn't restrict movement. Despite coming from a swimming background, I wasn't a strong kicker, so the wetsuit transition was relatively easy because you don't typically kick while wearing a wetsuit in open water.

When I got on the bike, I was in for another shock. The race setting, a car parking lot filled with tight corners and U-turns, demanded skills I had yet to develop fully, such as handling a road bike in draft-legal races and navigating sharp turns. In my recent book, I discuss my lingering nervousness when going downhill on a bike, a fear that hasn't entirely left me. Despite the anxiety and the "what ifs" that run through my mind, I focus on my why, the driving force that eclipses the fear.

Over time, riding in groups and even on a motorcycle helped me confront these fears, though they never entirely dissipated. Trusting in my skills and my bike became crucial to overcoming these challenges.

Winning the triathlon at the 2016 Olympics was a monumental achievement, yet my aspirations stretch beyond that. My journey from a high school project to the Olympic podium reflects my growth as an athlete and the enduring passion and perseverance that define my approach to triathlons.

CHAPTER 2

Understanding the Triathlon

"I meticulously prepared my transition area—towel, cleats, HOKAs, nutrition—and forgot my helmet." –Pathetic Triathlete Member

Triathlon is a multidiscipline sport that combines swimming, cycling, and running in one event. It's a test of endurance, strength, and strategy. It is also exciting and thrilling. Many people say that once you've experienced a triathlon, you can quickly get addicted.

Very few studies have examined who becomes a triathlete. However, from my observations, most triathletes have a background in running and cycling. Individuals with a swimming background may be at an advantage, as many triathletes consider swimming their weakest discipline. Whatever your strength, triathlon is accessible to all runners, cyclists, and swimmers.

As a beginner, understanding the structure and rules of a triathlon can be overwhelming. But with time and patience, you can do it.

Triathlon Distances

There are six primary distances in triathlon.

1. Super Sprint Distance is a great start for someone who wants to dip their toe in the water and see what a triathlon is like. The distances include a 400-meter swim (sometimes in the pool), a 10K (6.2 mile) bike, and a 2.5-mile run.

2. Sprint Distance is also an excellent starting point for beginners. It usually consists of a 750-meter swim, a 20K (12.4 mile) bike ride, and a 5K (3.1 mile) run. The swim and bike distances can vary. Some sprint triathlons have shorter swims, between 400 and 750 yards. The bike portion can also be shorter.

3. Olympic Distance is unlike the sprint triathlon because the distance doesn't deviate from one race to the next. The swim is 1.5K (0.93-mile swim),

the bike is 40K (24.8-miles), and the run is 10K (6.2-miles). This is a significant step up from a sprint distance race.

4. International Distance is like the Olympic triathlon, except that one of the segments may be shorter. For example, the swim may be shorter, the bike may be 30K instead of 40K, or the run can be a 5-mile run instead of a 6.2-mile run.

5. A Half-Distance Triathlon is a significant step up from the Olympic distance. You will complete a 1.2-mile swim, a 56-mile bike ride, and a 13.1-mile (half marathon) run. This is also known as a Half Ironman in an Ironman-branded event.

6. Full-Distance Triathlon is the ultimate endurance test. It involves a 2.4-mile swim, a 112-mile bike ride, and a 26.2-mile (full marathon) run. This is also known as an Ironman in an Ironman-branded event.

Transitions—T1 and T2

Every triathlon has transition areas where you set up your swim, bike, and run gear. In between each leg of the race, you return to the transition area, which is like your home base. Transitions are just as important as the disciplines themselves. They are referred to as T1 and T2.

T1, or Transition 1, is the transition from the swim to the bike. After the swim, athletes enter the transition area to put on their cycling gear. This includes removing the wetsuit and swim gear, putting on bike shoes and helmets, and grabbing their bike.

T2, or Transition 2, is the transition from the bike to the run. After completing the bike portion, athletes return to the transition area, rack their bikes, remove their helmets, and change into running shoes. The bike must be racked first before

taking off your helmet. If you don't, you could get a disqualification (DQ).

Transition times are included in your total race time, so efficiency is key. Practice your transitions during training to make them as smooth and quick as possible.

Dressing for a Triathlon

One common question among beginners is, "Do you wear the same clothes for all three disciplines?" The answer is yes.

Most triathletes wear a tri kit, versatile clothing for swimming, cycling, and running. Tri kits come in one- or two-piece sets made from quick-drying, flexible materials that allow for a wide range of movement. They also have a small, built-in pad or chamois for added comfort during the bike ride. The difference between a one- and two-piece tri kit is that the two-piece is easier to take off to go to the bathroom, whereas the one-piece is more aerodynamic.

However, for added comfort, some athletes may change clothes during transitions, especially during longer-distance races like a full-distance triathlon. A full-distance triathlon typically sets up tents for men and women to change their clothing. This is especially critical when the weather is inclement.

Changing your clothing during a shorter race is unnecessary, but some people do it, which adds to your time. The choice ultimately depends on personal preference and the specific race conditions.

When I did the Key West Triathlon, a beginner triathlete wore underwear under his wetsuit. When he got to transition, he removed the wetsuit and changed into his bike shorts. I would not recommend this, as it adds a lot of time to the overall event.

Understanding how a triathlon works is the first step toward preparing for your race. Familiarize yourself with the distances and the transition process, and practice wearing your tri kit during training.

QUICK TIPS

- Start with a sprint or a super sprint triathlon. Get the feel of racing first before embarking on a longer distance.
- Buy a triathlon kit, either one piece or two, and get used to wearing it while training and racing.

CHAPTER 3

Eight Basic Rules of Triathlon

"I got lost at one of these run-bike-runs, probably my first. The run was a loop, but the second run was done in the opposite direction. There was a branch in the path I hadn't noticed on the first lap, and I managed to go the wrong way. By the time I figured it out, people had started looking for me." –WeREndurance Member

USAT is our governing body. Like every governing body, it has rules you must follow when you race in a triathlon.

Rule 1

You must wear your helmet and chinstraps before unracking the bike in T1. When you return the bike to T2, rack it before removing the helmet and chin straps.

Rule 2

Only authorized personnel, including volunteers or medical staff, can assist with hydration, gels, a towel, or anything else.

Rule 3

All athletes must ride on the right and pass on the left (in a US-based event). It is courtesy to shout out, "On your left." This lets the cyclist know that you are passing them. You will get a penalty if a race official sees you passing on the right. You cannot draft either. This means getting close to the cyclist in front of you, creating a slipstream or area of lower air pressure behind them. This makes it easier for the follower to maintain speed with less effort, as they experience less aerodynamic drag. If you are close, pass the cyclist. Otherwise, you may get a penalty, which could be added time to your race. Or it could get you disqualified.

Rule 4

All athletes must complete the entire course in order.

Rule 5

You are not allowed to wear headphones or have a communication device. You can carry a phone, but only use it if you take yourself off the course. This is grounds for a DQ.

Rule 6

There are no glass containers on the course.

Rule 7

You must wear the race numbers during the entire race. Numbers can be in the form of a race tattoo or an indelible marker. The timing chip is typically worn on your ankle and must be worn throughout the race. In addition, the race number bib must be seen during the run and belongs in front of you, not behind you.

Rule 8

Once you receive your race number, you cannot give it to someone else, even if you cannot race. The penalty includes a DQ plus a 1-year suspension from USA Triathlon.

All triathlon races require a USAT card/number. I suggest buying one for a year at a time, but you can also purchase one for the day of the event only.

QUICK TIPS

- Follow the rules set by the USAT governing body.
- Make sure you understand the rules before you race. For other rules and regulations, visit the USAT website.

Hilary J. M. Topper
Triathlete, Author of *From Couch Potato to Endurance Athlete*, Triathlon/Swim/Run Coach, Merrick, NY

My alarm went off at 4 a.m. I jumped out of bed at the South Seas Island Resort in Captiva, Florida, and started to put on my race gear. I braided my hair and was ready by 4:15 a.m., so I started the coffee pot. Becky, my training partner, was still sleeping. I heard her alarm go off, and she exited the bedroom. "You're up already and ready to go?" she asked.

We discussed being at the transition area at 5:15 a.m. Although it closed at 6:45 a.m., we wanted ample time to set up and prepare for the big day. This was our first triathlon, and we didn't know what to expect.

We left the house at 5 a.m. and rode our bicycles about a mile and a half in the pitch black without bike lights to the race site. Some cars passed us, and they offered temporary lighting, but for the most part, we rode in the dark. It was pretty scary.

When we got to the transition area, we walked in and looked for our spots. I was number #616, and Becky was #508, so we were in different sections. I found my allocated space, racked the bike, and set up transition. There were a lot of first-timers there, so their stuff was all over the place. Some people spread out, while others were compact. Some had their gear in the front of the bikes, while others had it at the rear. I wanted to do it right, so I put mine compactly by the bike's front wheel.

After I finished, I went to find Becky. I wanted to make one more pit stop at the bathroom and borrow her flip-flops. After using the porta-potty, I heard my number called. "Number #616, please report to your bike."

I dropped off Becky's flip-flops and ran to my bike. "You're not in the right spot," said one of the women. "You're in the wrong area." I was racking my bike at 416 instead of 616.

I got a bit frantic. I ran around looking for my spot, and I found it. I pulled my bike off the rack and returned to get all my gear. Becky saw me and helped me set up.

After I was settled, Becky said, "Let's go to the water and warm up before the race."

So, we both went barefoot and followed the crowd to the water. We stepped on shells and other hard objects. My feet were raw, and the event hadn't even started yet!

When we reached the water, about a quarter of a mile away, we put on our swim caps and entered the water. I had a pink one, and she had a white one because we were in different age groups. I swam out to the first buoy, about 50 yards, and back. I wanted to make sure I could do this. I did it without a hitch and felt confident, even though the last buoy looked far away.

The elite racers were off first, followed by the white caps, Becky's group. A few more groups entered the water before the pink caps entered. When the horn blew, everyone with the pink caps ran into the water. It was insane. It was like nothing I had seen before. It felt as if everyone was in a panic. People were throwing their arms all over the place. People were kicking and punching me as I swam, but I didn't let that bother me. I was kicking and punching people, too. There were many people in the water, but I felt safe. There were plenty of lifeguards there, too.

As I swam, I kept thinking I could do this. I didn't stop. I kept moving my arms and kicking my legs. The first buoy came and went. I had one more to go. I could do this, I thought to myself. I got this. I kept thinking about what my coach said: "Just swim, take it easy, and breathe. Don't panic."

I tried to stay calm and relaxed. Finally, I reached the last buoy and turned toward the beach. I swam until I felt the bottom, stood up, and ran out of the water. A lot of people were cheering us on. I stayed focused and got to T1 as soon as possible.

I ran into the transition area and found my bike and gear. I dried off my feet, threw on my bicycle shoes, put on my helmet and glasses, picked up the bike from the rack, and was off. I tried to run out of the transition area the way my coach showed me. I got to the mount line, got on my bike, and rode 5 miles down a winding road. There were some sharp turns on the road, and when we got to mile 5, there was a sharp U-turn. Many men passed me during this race section, screaming, "On your left." Some came so close to me that I thought my bike would fall over. I felt like I was in the Tour de France (or maybe they thought they were!).

I was trying to go as fast as I could. I couldn't gauge my speed because the bike had no cadence sensor, so I just tried to follow people. I kept spotting the same man in a white T-shirt. I passed him, he passed me, and we kept going back and forth. I tried to keep up with his cadence and go faster when I was behind him.

The roads were bumpy and rough. My bottom wasn't happy, but I kept going. I didn't even want to reach for my water bottle for fear of slowing down!

As I approached the dismount line, I unclipped my pedals and rode the bike back into the transition area for T2.

I quickly found my spot, removed my gear, put on my sneakers and racing belt, and was off. There were tons of people walking out of T2 to the run, which slowed me down. I wanted to be able to run the full distance, but found that between my breathing and my aches and pains, I had to walk a little. I wasn't alone; there were plenty of walkers.

We ran around a golf course twice. The terrain differed from what I was used to—gravel, stone, and sand. The course was rolling and hilly, going up and down. There was no shade, and it was getting very hot. During that first mile, I focused on my kids and how much they meant to me. They both were so supportive during this training process, and their belief in me, got me through mile 2.

I walked a little after mile 2. A 35-year-old man was also walking. I encouraged him to run when I felt my breathing was more in control. We started to talk a little. We got each other through the end of the race and to the finish line, where I threw up my arms and screamed, "I did it!"

To this day, it is one of the most emotional races I have ever competed in. When I crossed the finish line, I was given a medal and a cold towel. I looked for Becky, but I didn't see her. I knew she was ahead of me, so I headed to the transition area and thought she could still be there.

I decided to wait. In the meantime, I called my coach and told him about the experience.

"Did you call your family yet?" he asked.

"No, you were the first one I called because you're my coach," I said. "And anyway, everyone in my house is probably sleeping!"

He congratulated me and told me he was proud of my accomplishment.

I finally found Becky. We went over to see how we did and discovered we were only 3 minutes apart. We hugged and expressed that completing our first triathlon together was amazing!

Adapted from the book, *From Couch Potato to Endurance Athlete: A Portrait of a Non-Athletic Triathlete*, published by Meyer & Meyer Sport.

CHAPTER 4

Every Shape, Every Size: Embracing Diversity in Triathlon

"During the run, at a very hot Ironman race, I passed two women and heard one say, 'I don't know why I keep signing up for these damn things.'" –Pathetic Triathlete Member

When I started training for triathlons, I thought all triathletes had muscular bodies. I was overweight, but I trained a lot. I remember one of my family members saying, "I don't understand. You train constantly, yet you are still chubby."

Triathlon is a sport that celebrates diversity and inclusivity. It's a community where athletes of every shape, size, age, race, and ability come together to push their limits and achieve their personal best. The myth that there's a "one-size-fits-all" body type for triathletes needs to be debunked.

Breaking the Stereotype

When you think of an athlete, you might picture someone lean, muscular, and seemingly chiseled from stone. While it's true that many professional and elite athletes have these characteristics, it's important to remember that they represent only a fraction of the athletic community. The reality is that athletes come in all shapes and sizes, and this diversity is one of the sport's greatest strengths.

Body Diversity in Triathlon

Triathlon requires a balance of strength, endurance, and agility. Athletes may have different body types depending on their strengths and weaknesses in these disciplines. Some may be leaner with strong cardiovascular endurance, while others may have more muscle mass for power and speed. The key is to understand your body and train it accordingly.

Your body is your vehicle in this sport, capable of incredible things regardless of size or shape. Refrain from comparing yourself to others; focus on your journey and progress. This is hard to do. When I first started, I compared myself to everyone. But by doing that, I lessened my impact on myself and the community.

Embracing Your Unique Athletic Identity

As a beginner triathlete, embracing your unique athletic identity is crucial. Recognize that your body type doesn't define your potential—your determination, discipline, and passion for the sport genuinely matter.

Train to your strengths and work on your weaknesses. Listen to your body. Give it the fuel and rest it needs to perform at its best. The goal isn't to fit into a specific mold but to become the best version of yourself as an athlete.

Jamesport Triathlon, Long Island, NY. Came in third place for the Aquabike.

Inclusivity and Community

The triathlon community is one of inclusivity and encouragement. It's a sport where athletes cheer each other on, regardless of their body type, fitness level, race, color of their skin, sexual orientation, and nationality. You belong here, whether you're a seasoned triathlete or just starting.

Athena and Clydesdale Divisions

In the United States, you can compete in an Athena division for women and a Clydesdale division for men. In this division, you will compete against people who weigh around the same as you. The Clydesdale division is for male athletes weighing more than 220 pounds. The Athena division is for female athletes weighing more than 165 pounds.

Triathlon is a sport for everyone. Embrace your unique athletic identity, train hard, and most importantly, enjoy the journey. After all, it's not just about crossing the finish line—it's your journey of self-discovery and growth.

QUICK TIPS

- Embrace who you are. No matter if you are overweight or underweight, you belong here.
- There are all body types in triathlon. Don't be ashamed or embarrassed. We are one big family here.

CHAPTER 5

Finding the Right Race

"First tri . . . started the open water swim and did ok for the first 100 yards. When a swimmer hit me several times, I panicked and flipped to backstroke to calm down. I tried to return to freestyle and panicked again, but got disoriented in the middle of a triangle lake course. After throwing up in the middle of the lake, I decided to backstroke the rest. The kayak stopped me twice because I was going the opposite way. She stayed by my side, tapping my leg as I veered off course. Finally, I got on land only to throw up again due to stress. But I did finish the race and have settled into enjoying the open water more." –Pathetic Triathlete Member

So many people tell me they want to compete in a triathlon but don't know where to start. Many first-timers sign up for a half- or full-distance triathlon as their first race. I wouldn't advise that. I suggest everyone start with a super sprint or a sprint triathlon and then build from there.

Many people think that "Ironman" is synonymous with triathlon. It is not. Competing in an Ironman is only for some. Don't "pooh-pooh" sprint and Olympic races. They are tough, but with proper training, you can get there.

What should you look for when signing up for your first race?

For starters, evaluate your fitness level. Be honest with yourself. Are you consistent in your training?

Consider the terrain. Is the racecourse flat or hilly? Is it in open water (like a lake or ocean) or a pool? If you live near hills and enjoy cycling up them, a hilly bike course is the thing for you. An open-water swim might be more appealing if you're a strong swimmer.

Depending on where you live, triathlons can take place all year round, but many people find it easier to train for and race in events that take place in the summer or fall. This is especially true if the event includes an open-water swim, as the water is warmer in June than in April in the northeast.

Location is also important. Is there a race close to home that would make logistics easier? Or do you see this as an opportunity for a fun travel experience? Both can work. Remember that traveling to a race adds another layer of complexity to your preparations. I did my first triathlon in Florida. Traveling from New York caused a lot of unnecessary stress because of all the extra gear you need to bring.

Do you have time to train? Pick a race that is far enough in the future so that you have ample time to prepare for it. If you're starting from a base of good general fitness, a standard recommendation is to allow at least 12–16 weeks to train for a sprint distance triathlon. However, 20 weeks is a good place to start so that you can work on your deficiencies.

Ask around for recommendations. If you know other triathletes, consider contacting them or joining some Facebook groups. There are tons of Facebook groups for triathletes. Other athletes can offer valuable insights and may be able to recommend particularly beginner-friendly races.

The vibe is also important. Some races are known for being friendly, fun, and welcoming to newcomers. Others might be more competitive. While others have more community support cheering you on every step of the way. Which sounds like more fun to you?

Your goal for your first triathlon should be a positive experience. Choose a race that excites you, train well, remember your why, and have fun!

There are so many fantastic race companies across the country. Below are some I would recommend. However, make sure to Google them, as they may have merged and be under a different name by the time of publication.

- Alpha Win
- DelMoSports
- Epic Races
- EventPower LI
- Integrity Multisport
- Life Time Athletic Events
- Race Awesome
- Ripit Events

- Robert J. Aaron Memorial Mighty Montauk Triathlon
- St. Anthony's Triathlon
- Toughman Triathlon

There are hundreds and hundreds more races. Go to the USAT website and search for Triathlon Events and USAT Sanctioned Events. You will find a list of triathlons located in almost every area of the country. In addition, USAT holds National Champion Races throughout the country. Find out how you can participate at usatriathlon.org/events.

Try to support your local community race company. They need your help and usually do a fantastic job organizing an unforgettable triathlon.

QUICK TIPS

- Triathlons are fun but take serious work, whether you sign up for a sprint or a full-distance triathlon.
- Find a logistically feasible race. Remember, you have a lot of "stuff" to bring with you, so find a race that works for you.

Tim Snow
Managing Partner at QT2, Easton, MA

My introduction to triathlons began at the Sharon Triathlon event in the quaint town adjacent to my childhood home in Massachusetts. I was 22, nursing a running injury from my college days. As a result, I had taken up swimming before school and purchased a bike from Sears for $179, naively bypassing a superior model for an extra $20.

A significant influence on my triathlon journey was pro triathlete, Karen Smyers, who the women's track team coach invited to share her experiences with the women's and men's teams. Karen stated that anyone who could run and swim could easily pick up biking and participate in a triathlon. Her words resonated with me, as I was swimming sidestroke a mile a day in 33 minutes.

Influenced by her talk, I registered for a local triathlon a few weeks later, barely a day or two before the event. I had a mountain bike, but it wasn't until the day prior that I realized I needed a helmet, which led to a quick shopping trip.

When race day arrived, I plunged into it wearing soccer shorts. The ½-mile swim, 12.4-mile bike ride, and 4.4-mile run were more challenging than anticipated. After the swim, as I transitioned to the mountain bike, I realized I couldn't maintain the pace I had started with. Watching other athletes whizz past me on their triathlon bikes was a humbling experience.

Emerging from the bike leg of the race, I found myself far behind the pack. However, my cocky 22-year-old self had arrived at the race expecting to win! That didn't happen, but I felt invincible as I started the run, passing other competitors rapidly. This exhilarating feeling was addictive and propelled me toward a 26-year career as a triathlete. Despite finishing in 165th place that day, I was hooked and started racing every weekend.

What began as a passion morphed into a career. From 2000 to 2013, I held my pro card and participated in around 45 to 50 Ironman events. The highlight of this journey was returning to the Sharon Triathlon 25 years later. At 47, I not only participated but also won the entire race. This full-circle moment was a hard-fought victory and an incredibly fulfilling experience.

CHAPTER 6

Do You Need a Triathlon Coach?

"I started the second run wearing my bike helmet during a run-bike-run practice session." –WeREndurance Member

When I started training for a triathlon, I immediately hired a coach. But I didn't initially understand why I had to. My running partner said, "It's important."

I interviewed a few coaches and went with a man in his 30s who lived an hour away from me. He invited me to various group activities, and even though I went, I didn't fit in. The athletes he coached seemed way over my skill level. I was a beginner, and everything seemed challenging, including buying a bathing suit!

Although I am now a triathlon coach, I still love interacting with a coach. I enjoy talking with someone about my workouts, and I like to be held accountable, and a coach helps me achieve that.

A good coach can structure your training, offer advice based on their experience, and help you avoid common pitfalls. But how do you find the right coach?

Before starting your search, understand what you need from a coach. Are you a beginner needing to learn the basics of each discipline? Or are you an experienced athlete aiming to improve your performance? Your answer will determine the level of expertise you should seek in a coach.

Should you buy a plan or work with a coach? Purchasing a plan is easy. Some people buy them on Training Peaks, while others purchase specific books, like this one or Matt Fitzgerald's book, *80/20 Triathlon*. His training advice is to do 80% of your efforts at an easy volume and 20% at a hard interval. However, books and plans don't offer support like a coach will.

Ensure potential coaches, such as a Level 1 Certified Triathlon Coach, have relevant qualifications. The USAT, Ironman University, and the

International Triathlon Union (ITU) offer coaching certification programs. These certifications indicate that a coach has received formal education in triathlon training principles and that the training is rigorous.

The basic certification is a Level 1 USAT coach. This well-rounded individual has completed two full days in class, passed a 100-question quiz, and needs to continue their education by getting a certain number of Continuing Education Unit credits every two years to be re-certified.

A Level 2 USAT coach specializes in short-course, long-course, youth, or para-athlete coaching.

A Level 3 USAT coach focuses on coaching elite and professional athletes.

Experience matters, both as a coach and as an athlete. Even mediocre athletes can make great coaches. Many people think that being an Olympian or an elite triathlete makes one a better coach than an age-group athlete, but that's not true. Although they may be great athletes, it doesn't make them great coaches or someone to relate to.

Every coach has a unique style, and finding one that aligns with your personality and learning style is essential. Some coaches are more hands-on, while others may take a more laid-back approach. However, please note that coaches are not your workout buddies. They are there to oversee your training, not to do it with you. You need the motivation and will to do the work your coach outlines.

Some coaches may focus more on data, while others might emphasize the mental side of training. Try to meet potential coaches in person or talk to them over the phone to understand their style. Only some coaches will be the right fit, and you may need to try out many different coaches to find the right one.

My first coach trained me like a professional triathlete, but it was too intense and too frequent for a beginner. Simultaneously, I had a coach who was supportive but only provided feedback on some workouts I completed on Training Peaks (which we will discuss in a later chapter). Then, I had another coach who commented on all of my workouts. Bottom line, find a style that resonates with you.

How often will the coach be available to answer your questions or adjust your training plan? I prefer it when a coach is responsive when I ask them to change the schedule or answer questions. Communication via email, phone calls, text messages, and/or in-person meetings is also worth asking a potential coach. Make sure their communication style and availability meet your expectations.

Every coach has a different philosophy regarding training for a triathlon. Some might focus on high-intensity interval training (HIIT), while others prioritize volume and endurance. Then there are some coaches who implement both HIIT and endurance. Ensure their approach aligns with your fitness level, time availability, and personal beliefs about training.

When I coach beginners, I start with the basics. Consistency is my top priority. Then, we incorporate speed and endurance training.

Coaching services can vary significantly in price depending on the coach's experience, the level of service, and your location. You can spend between $150 and $500 a month on coaching. Be sure to discuss fees upfront and understand what services are included. Is individualized training part of the coaching? Is there an additional fee?

Finding the right coach can make all the difference in your triathlon journey. It may take time and research, but the investment is well worth the payoff in terms of the progress you'll make toward your triathlon goals.

QUICK TIPS

- Do you need someone to hold you accountable and keep you on track with a scheduled program? If so, interview a coach.
- Can you work off a plan someone creates for you, but you don't need input? Then, buy one.

CHAPTER 7

Becoming Part of a Bigger Community

"I was once in a tri that had a half and full Ironman distance races on the same course with the same start. The swim was one loop for the half and two loops for the full. As I came out of the swim (for my one loop), everyone was cheering, ringing cowbells, and yelling that the first woman was out of the water for the full. (They thought I had done two loops.) So, as I was trying to wave them off and fess up that I was doing the half, the woman who was the first out of the water for the full ran by and began taking off her wetsuit with absolutely no fanfare at all."
–Pathetic Triathlete Member

The triathlon journey is filled with personal growth, challenges, and the joy of crossing the finish line. A pivotal step in this journey involves joining governing bodies like USAT and USMS. These organizations ensure a safe, structured, and competitive environment for triathletes and swimmers of all levels.

The Role of USA Triathlon

USAT is the national governing body for triathlon and other multisport disciplines in the US. It is dedicated to developing and promoting triathlon in the country and fostering a vibrant community of athletes, from beginners to seasoned professionals.

Why Join?

Before you race, you must have a membership with USAT. This ensures that all competitors are covered by insurance and adhere to standardized rules that promote fairness and safety. However, there are lots of other benefits, including:

- Insurance Coverage—Members receive accident insurance for injuries sustained during sanctioned events and official training sessions, providing peace of mind as you push your limits.
- Resources and Education—USAT offers a wealth of resources, including coaching services and educational content designed to enhance performance and enjoyment of the sport.

USAT Races

USAT sanctions thousands of races nationwide each year, catering to all levels of experience and ambition. From local sprint triathlons perfect for beginners to the prestigious USA Triathlon National Championships, there's a race for every athlete looking to challenge themselves and achieve their goals. The USA Triathlon National Championships are for those athletes who place in their age group during specific sanctioned races.

For example, my second race was an EventPower LI race in Montauk. I won my age group and was accepted to participate in the USA Triathlon National Championships the following year. This was an exciting, fun, and humbling experience.

The Importance of US Masters Swimming

Mastering the swim segment is often one of the biggest challenges for triathletes. Joining USMS can be a game-changer in improving one's swimming skills and confidence, especially in open water.

When I first started training, a USMS-sanctioned swim group called Masters Swimming taught me how to swim and improved my stroke. It helps to be in Masters Swimming to get a feel for what it's like to be in the pool with many people and in the open water. These conditions emulate race conditions and are helpful when race day comes.

Why Join USMS?

Here are some reasons:

Structured Training—Joining a Masters Swimming group provides access to structured workouts led by experienced coaches, which can help you improve technique, endurance, and speed.

Community and Support—Being part of a swim group means surrounding yourself with fellow swimmers who can offer advice, encouragement, and camaraderie.

Open-Water Safety—USMS membership often includes safety clinics and sanctioned open-water swims for those venturing into open water, ensuring you're well-prepared and protected.

Competitive Opportunities—USMS hosts various swimming events and competitions, offering a platform to test your progress and compete against others in your age group.

Membership Fees

USAT and USMS require an annual membership fee, which varies depending on the membership type (individual, family, etc.). These fees contribute to the organization's operational costs, including event sanctioning, insurance coverage, and member benefits. Look at each website for the current fees.

By joining USAT and USMS, you gain access to races and insurance and become part of a supportive community dedicated to helping you succeed in your multisport endeavors. Whether taking your first strokes in the pool or eyeing a spot at the national championships, these organizations provide the resources, opportunities, and inspiration needed to thrive in the challenging yet rewarding triathlon world.

QUICK TIP

- I suggest joining both USAT and USMS. The education and opportunities are worth the cost of membership. They communicate via email; you can find more information on their websites.

CHAPTER 8

829 69

Social Networks and Camaraderie

"A runner came prepared for wet grounds with sneakers that were loafers, perfect for protecting his feet from the wet, muddy ground. When it was time to start the race, he discovered that he had only packed one of his expensive running shoes, and the loafers were unsuitable. Luckily, he fished through the throwaway bins and found something better than the loafers." –WeREndurance Member

The triathlon is more than just a race. It's a community, a lifestyle, and a testament to the human spirit and its ceaseless pursuit of self-improvement. Most importantly, it's a shared journey. Although you train and race alone, no triathlete undertakes the journey alone. Behind every triathlete is an intricate web of networks.

Sometimes, family and friends provide the emotional support needed during this arduous journey. They cheer you on during races, offer encouragement when you're feeling low, and celebrate with you when you cross the finish line. There are times when your family isn't supportive. When that happens, you can get support from the triathlon community online and offline.

The Power of the Pack

Triathletes are a unique breed. We willingly subject ourselves to grueling training regimes and push our bodies to the limit. Yet, we do it with an unyielding spirit, fueled by the camaraderie within the triathlon community.

Training for a triathlon can be daunting. It involves hours of daily practice across three disciplines: swimming, cycling, and running. That is why I am motivated when someone posts about their training or triathlon experience on social media.

I also get motivated when I train with my training partners. Doing this helps me get up in the "wee" hours of the morning to train, knowing that someone is waiting for me.

Being part of a community makes the training burden lighter. Training sessions become social gatherings where you can swap stories, share tips, and motivate others to push your limits. Even if you train alone, seeing people you recognize from social media or the community makes a huge difference. It gives you a boost of confidence to go the extra mile.

For example, no matter which race I sign up for and compete in, I always meet people I know, whether from an online conversation or another triathlon team.

Social Networks

At the time of publication, triathletes are more active on Facebook and Instagram than other sites. Many private Facebook groups allow triathletes to chat with other triathletes, ask questions, and post photos of their training activities. I enjoy the Pathetic Triathlete group run by Bill Hoolihan, the founder of RaceDay. I also run a Triathlete's Diary group, and there are many first-time triathlete groups.

Some groups have private communities, like my WeREndurance Athletes group, where your training partners and coaches can provide technical guidance and motivation. The bonds formed with training partners often transcend the realms of sport and evolve into lifelong friendships.

Strava is an app for Android and iPhone that lets you view other people's workouts. You connect Strava to your smartwatch, and your followers can see your activities. If they like what you did, they'll give you "kudos" or leave a comment. Plus, you can share photos of your workouts. There are also challenges to join, and you can be part of your triathlon team to get inspired by others' workouts.

I love meeting people at events, and I have spoken to them on social media and Strava. It feels good to see them in person because they are my support system. I often find myself hugging these folks, even though I barely know them offline. You do build friendships online.

Success in triathlons is about more than physical fitness. It's about being part of a community that shares your passion, understands your struggles, and celebrates your victories. It's about embracing the spirit of camaraderie and harnessing the power of social networks. Because in the world of triathlons, no one succeeds alone.

QUICK TIP

- Make sure to join a triathlon support group on Facebook. There are dozens of groups, and each offers invaluable information. Here, you can ask questions or post photos from training and racing.

Gina Cornell
Triathlete, Wausau, WI

My triathlon journey began at the Marathon City Ultra Mini triathlon, a beginner-friendly event with two sprint distances: a competitive traditional sprint and a shorter super sprint. I got excited when I spotted a poster advertising a charity triathlon in a neighboring town. My knowledge of triathlons was limited to the iconic image of Julie Moss crawling across the finish line.

I swam in high school and enjoyed cycling. I felt confident enough to tackle a ⅛-mile swim, a 5-K bike ride, and a ½-mile run, so my husband and I signed up.

The Ultra Mini super sprint was self-timed, and despite considering myself fit, I found the swimming portion challenging. The bike ride seemed endlessly long, and my face was a vivid tomato red when we reached the run. Yet, crossing that finish line to cheers from the crowd made me determined to try again.

I recruited a friend the following year, and we both entered the sprint. As we stood by the pool, doubt crept in, but there was no turning back.

The race organizers knew it was my first time and warned us about the hilly terrain. The most daunting part was a steep hill just before the running segment. At that point, a truck pulled beside me and asked if he could return my bike to the course. He saw me struggling. But I refused, determined to finish, knowing I was the last person on the course.

As I entered transition, I saw numerous participants had showered and were heading to the awards ceremony. Meanwhile, I had a hilly 5K ahead. Despite the challenge, I completed it. Seeing the race organizer cry joyfully at my perseverance was incredibly touching.

Finishing last was a blow to my ego, but the support from friends and the race organizer made it all worthwhile. Plus, delicious lemon bars were waiting at the finish line!

The key takeaway from this experience is that finishing last doesn't matter. The real achievement is in finishing the race, and that's what truly counts.

CHAPTER 9

Consistency

"For my first sprint triathlons, I did not own a wetsuit. When I began shopping for one, I found one on Sam's Club's website for only $60. I didn't know what I was doing, so naturally, I wore my new 'jet skiing' wetsuit backward. I wish I could find the photos." –WeREndurance Member

Consistency

During my 10-plus years as a triathlete, I realized that consistency is the key to achieving one's goals. It helps build a solid endurance base, essential for becoming faster and more efficient in your sport.

But it's hard to be consistent when you first start. Your mind will tell you it's unnecessary, and you will often listen. But don't listen unless your body tells you to stop.

The first step toward achieving consistency is understanding why you're doing this. This will help motivate you to stick to your training regimen and goals. (This goes back to the why in chapter 1.)

Consistent and frequent training sessions, even short and easy, can be more beneficial than infrequent, intense workouts. I have coached athletes who don't do anything all week and then take the daily schedule and try to fit it all in on the weekend. That doesn't work. Instead, pick a time that works for you and stick to it.

My training routine consists of:

- I put out my clothes the night before and prepare my hydration by storing it in the refrigerator.
- I wake up at 4 a.m., take my vitamins and supplements, and then drink a cup of coffee.
- I leave by 5 a.m., ready to start my 5:30 a.m. workout.

I love to train in the morning before I start my day. If I don't do it in the morning, it won't happen. I'll get bogged down in many other things, and before I know it, it's time for dinner. Others like to work out after work. Whatever fits your schedule, do it.

In addition, train according to the specific demands of your race. A consistent training routine will help improve your endurance, but may not improve your speed. You can incorporate speed into your training, which we will discuss later. Interval training is the best way to get faster.

Consistency in endurance sports happens only over time. It's a gradual process that requires patience, determination, and discipline.

QUICK TIPS

- Try to be as consistent as possible. Get something in every day, even if it's for 30 minutes.
- I suggest early morning activities before the family awakens. The night before, prepare your clothes and hydration. When you wake up, get out and go.
- This will help you build your base for your first or next triathlon.

CHAPTER 10

Understanding Training Zones in Triathlon

"I signed up for an Ironman event. When I got there, I prepared myself and did the swim. When I got to T1, I was so excited that I was talking with everyone there. Suddenly, I was all alone, and someone tapped me on the shoulder to tell me that the transition was closing in 30 seconds. I ended up DNFing the bike." –WeREndurance Member

Training zones are a fundamental concept in triathlon training. They refer to different levels of intensity at which you can train. Each zone focuses on physical changes, making you stronger, faster, and more efficient.

The most accurate way to determine your training zones is through a lab-based VO_2 max or lactate threshold test. However, these tests can be expensive and inaccessible. A more practical method is to use field tests, such as a time trial or a maximum heart rate test, and then calculate your zones based on the results.

Training zones are typically divided into five main categories, each corresponding to a certain percentage of your maximum heart rate (MHR), power output, or pace. To determine your MHR, use this formula: 211 – (0.64 × Age).

Zone 1 (Recovery) is the lowest intensity level, usually below 60% of MHR. Training in this zone aids recovery, promotes fat burning, and helps build an aerobic base.

- Swim: Slow, easy laps focusing on form and technique rather than speed.
- Bike: Leisurely cycling at a comfortable pace where you can easily carry on a conversation.
- Run: A relaxed jog or an easy walk/run interval (like a 15-second run/30-second walk).

Zone 2 (Aerobic Endurance) is where you'll spend most of your training time, usually between 60% and 70% of MHR. It's comfortable enough to hold a conversation, yet it improves aerobic fitness, endurance, and fat-burning capacity.

- Swim: Steady-paced swims, focusing on consistent speed and efficiency over longer distances.
- Bike: Moderate rides, maintaining a steady pace where talking in complete sentences is possible but requires some effort.

- Run: This is easy-to-moderate-paced running where you can speak a few sentences simultaneously. The goal is consistent effort and building an aerobic base.

Zone 3 (Tempo) is a moderate intensity, usually between 70% and 80% of MHR. Training in this zone improves aerobic capacity and efficiency.

- Swim: Swimming at a challenging yet sustainable pace, focusing on building endurance and speed.
- Bike: Tempo rides at a "comfortably hard" pace, pushing yourself harder than Zone 2 but still able to utter short phrases.
- Run: Steady runs where speaking is possible but difficult, ideal for improving race pace and metabolic efficiency.

Zone 4 (Threshold) is usually between 80% and 90% of MHR. Training here improves the lactate threshold, where lactic acid accumulates faster than it can be cleared, causing fatigue.

- Swim: Intervals or sets quickly, pushing close to maximum effort with short rest periods in between.
- Bike: Hard efforts at or near lactate threshold, where talking is limited to a word or two; often involves interval training.
- Run: Fast-paced intervals or hill repeats, focusing on pushing the pace shy of all-out effort, with recovery periods.

Zone 5 (Anaerobic or VO_2 Max) is the highest intensity level, usually above 90% of MHR. It's very challenging and can only be sustained for short periods. Training in this zone improves anaerobic capacity, power, and speed.

- Swim: Very high-intensity intervals with full-effort sprints, focusing on maximum speed and power for short durations.
- Bike: Short, intense intervals at maximum effort to improve power and speed, with complete recovery between efforts.
- Run: Sprints or short, very hard efforts to increase speed and power, focusing on maximal exertion with longer rest.

You can also use the Rate of Perceived Effort (RPE) with your MHR. This is a way to measure how hard you feel like you're working during physical activity. Instead of using devices or tests, you rely on your sense of effort.

Here's how it works: Imagine a scale from 0 to 10.

- 0 means no effort at all, like sitting in a chair
- 1-2 is a very light effort, like a slow walk
- 3-4 is moderate effort, where you can talk comfortably but feel like you're exercising
- 5-6 is somewhat hard; you can still speak, but with more effort
- 7-8 is hard; talking becomes difficult
- 9-10 is very hard to maximal effort, where you're giving it your all and can't maintain it for long

Using RPE, you can manage your workouts based on how you feel rather than relying solely on heart rate or pace. This helps you listen to your body and adjust your intensity as needed.

Time Trials

Here are some time trials you can use to determine your training zones. These should be used along with the MHR zones.

Swimming

Warm-Up: Start with a 10-minute easy swim, including drills and short sprints to prepare your muscles.

Main Set: Swim a 1,000- or 1,500-yard time trial at the most sustainable pace. Record the time it takes to complete this distance.

Cool-Down: Finish with a 5-10-minute easy swim to help your body recover.

(As an alternative, Matt Fitzgerald's *80/20 Triathlon* includes a variation of a time trial at 200/400/200 yards. This can assess your speed and endurance over a shorter period. Interestingly, TriDot also uses this method to calculate your pace.)

To calculate training zones, calculate your pace per 100 yards/meters:
Time / Distance × 100 = pace per 100 yards/meters
Example: If you swam 1,000 yards in 10 minutes, 10 / 1,000 × 100 = 1 minute per 100 yards/meters.

Determine your zones based on your pace per 100:

- Zone 1 (Recovery/Easy): 20-30 seconds slower than your time trial pace per 100
- Zone 2 (Endurance): 10-20 seconds slower than your time trial pace per 100
- Zone 3 (Moderate): 5-10 seconds slower than your time trial pace per 100
- Zone 4 (Threshold/Race Pace): Your time trial pace per 100
- Zone 5 (VO_2 Max/Speed): Faster than your time trial pace per 100

Example: If your time trial pace is 1:40 per 100 yards, your zones might look like this:

- Zone 1: 2:00-2:10 per 100 yards
- Zone 2: 1:50-2:00 per 100 yards
- Zone 3: 1:45-1:50 per 100 yards
- Zone 4: 1:40 per 100 yards
- Zone 5: Faster than 1:40 per 100 yards

Cycling

Warm-Up: Begin with a 15–20-minute easy ride, gradually increasing the intensity. To prepare your body, include a few 1-minute efforts at a high intensity.

Main Set: Find a steady, moderate hill. Start a 3–5-minute effort at a high intensity, aiming to reach your maximum effort at the last minute and safely pushing yourself as hard as you can. This is crucial to identifying your MHR.

An alternative to this could be a 20-minute time trial. After the warm-up, push for 20 minutes to sustain yourself. For the last 5 minutes, go as hard as you can.

Cool-Down: End with at least 10 minutes of easy cycling to help your body recover.

Calculating Time Trial Results: Measure Your MHR: Use a monitor to track your heart rate during the main set. The highest number you see during the final minute of the effort will be close to your MHR.

Use your MHR to determine training zones:
- Zone 1 (Recovery): 50–60% of MHR
- Zone 2 (Endurance): 60–70% of MHR
- Zone 3 (Tempo): 70–80% of MHR
- Zone 4 (Threshold): 80–90% of MHR
- Zone 5 (VO_2 Max): 90–100% of MHR

Example calculation: If your MHR recorded during the effort is 180 beats per minute (bpm), your training zones would be:
- Zone 1: 90–108 bpm
- Zone 2: 108–126 bpm
- Zone 3: 126–144 bpm
- Zone 4: 144–162 bpm
- Zone 5: 162–180 bpm

Running

Warm-Up: Jog for 15 minutes, including dynamic stretches and a few accelerations to prime your body.

Main Set: Run a one-mile time trial on a track or a familiar, flat route. Push yourself to the maximum sustainable pace. Monitor your heart rate throughout, especially noting the highest rate toward the end, to estimate your max heart rate.

An alternative would be to run a 5K. Like the 20-minute time trial listed under cycling, this will help you determine your sustainability and heart rate over that period.

Cool-Down: Cap off with a 10-minute easy jog or walk to aid recovery.

Calculate Your Average Pace: Record the total time it took to run the one mile. Divide the total time by the distance (one mile) to get your average pace per mile.

Example: If you ran 1 mile in 8 minutes, your pace is 8:00 per mile.

Determine Your MHR:

Your MHR will be approximated by the highest heart rate you recorded during the run, especially toward the end of the effort.

Using your results to determine training zones:

- Easy/Recovery Pace: 1:30–2:00 minutes slower than your time trial pace
- Endurance Pace: 1:00–1:30 minutes slower than your time trial pace
- Tempo Pace: 0:30–1:00 minutes slower than your time trial pace
- Threshold Pace: 0:00–0:30 seconds slower than your time trial pace
- Interval Pace: At or faster than your time trial pace

Heart rate-based training zones (using your MHR):

- Zone 1 (Recovery): 50–60% of MHR
- Zone 2 (Endurance): 60–70% of MHR
- Zone 3 (Tempo): 70–80% of MHR
- Zone 4 (Threshold): 80–90% of MHR
- Zone 5 (VO_2 Max): 90–100% of MHR

Example calculations:
If your 1-mile time was 8 minutes (8:00 pace) and your MHR was 180 bpm, your zones would be:

- Easy/Recovery Pace: 9:30–10:00 per mile
- Endurance Pace: 9:00–9:30 per mile
- Tempo Pace: 8:30–9:00 per mile
- Threshold Pace: 8:00–8:30 per mile
- Interval Pace: Faster than 8:00 per mile

Heart rate-based training zones:

- Zone 1: 90–108 bpm
- Zone 2: 108–126 bpm
- Zone 3: 126–144 bpm
- Zone 4: 144–162 bpm
- Zone 5: 162–180 bpm

Applying Training Zones to Your Triathlon Training

Training in different zones serves different purposes. For example, long, slow-distance workouts (Zones 1 and 2) build endurance, while HIIT workouts (Zones 4 and 5) boost speed and power.

Your training program should include workouts in all zones, but the distribution will depend on your goals, fitness level, and where you are in your training cycle. Typically, most training is done in Zones 1 and 2, with smaller amounts in the higher zones. However, when you are doing interval training, you will be in the higher zones.

Training zones are a tool to guide your training, but they're not set in stone. Listen to your body and adjust as needed. If you're feeling fatigued, it's okay to back off, even if your plan says otherwise. Similarly, if you're feeling strong, it's okay to push a little harder sometimes.

Ultimately, understanding and effectively using training zones can be a game-changer in triathlon training, allowing you to train more efficiently and achieve your goals.

QUICK TIPS

- Do a time trial once you have been consistent for at least a month or two. Then, figure out your MHR.
- Know your zones to see improvements throughout your training. I recommend testing yourself with a time trial every other month. As you get better, you will see improvements.

CHAPTER 11

Tracking Your Progress With Technology

"After being told wetsuits weren't necessary, I left my goggles and earplugs back in the car. I had to swim the entire distance with my head out of the water." –WeREndurance Member

Tracking your progress is essential to seeing improvements. Various devices, including power meters, Garmin multisport watches, heart rate monitors, and cadence sensors, offer in-depth insights into your performance. These tools can help you identify strengths and weaknesses, set goals, and gauge your progress.

Heart Rate Monitors

Heart rate monitors measure your heart rate in real time, providing instant feedback on your effort level. As discussed earlier, training in different heart rate zones can help you work on various aspects of your fitness.

A heart rate monitor can track your progress by monitoring changes in your resting heart rate (RHR) and heart rate recovery. A lower RHR often indicates improved cardiovascular fitness, and faster heart rate recovery, which shows improved fitness recovery. When I train, I wear an external heart rate monitor. Although my watch calculates my heart rate, it's not as accurate as an external monitor.

Finding your heart rate zones is important for training effectively. These zones are based on a percentage of your MHR. They help you understand the intensity of your workouts and tailor them to meet your specific fitness goals.

As discussed in the prior chapter, you can calculate your MHR by taking 211 - (0.64 × Age). So, for example, if you are 35, your MHR is 188.6.

Calculate Your RHR - Your RHR is your heart rate when completely resting. For the most accurate measurement, check your pulse before leaving bed first thing in the morning.

Calculate Your Heart Rate Reserve (HRR) - Your HRR is the difference between your MHR and RHR. To find this number, subtract your RHR from your MHR. For example, if your MHR is 175 and your RHR is 65, your HRR would be 110.

Some coaches might use the HRR to calculate the zones for individualized training programs. Each zone is defined as a range of percentages of your HRR added to your RHR. An easy workout may be in Zone 1, whereas a moderate workout will fluctuate between Zones 2 and 3.

These calculations provide estimates, and individual heart rate zones can vary. It is always a good idea to consult a medical expert before starting a new training program.

Garmin Multisport Watches

Many multisport watches, including Apple, Polar, and others, are on the market. However, during my tenure in the sport, I found that Garmin is my favorite. That may change, but as of 2025, their multisport watches are versatile tools for tracking various activities. They are equipped with GPS, heart rate monitors, and various other sensors to provide a comprehensive overview of your performance. Garmin far exceeds Apple Watch regarding more accurate fitness metrics, battery life, and in-depth sleep analysis.

They aren't cheap investments, but they are well worth the price. Garmin multisport watches range from $300 to $1,000, depending on which model you choose. Sometimes, you can buy a refurbished or used Garmin watch on Facebook. They last a long time!

One way to track your progress is by monitoring your VO_2 max, a measure of your body's maximal oxygen consumption during intense exercise. Garmin watches estimate your VO_2 max based on heart rate data and running speed. A higher VO_2 max indicates better cardiovascular fitness.

Another valuable metric Garmin watches provide is "Training Status," which tells you whether your training is productive, maintaining, peaking, overreaching, or detraining. This helps you ensure your training is practical and allows you to adjust your regimen if necessary. However, it's not always 100% accurate, so you are better off going by feel. If you need a break, listen to your body.

Another thing I like about Garmin is that if a particular workout is placed on Training Peaks (an online scheduler) or TriDot (an AI-generated app), it will automatically appear on your Garmin. You can choose to do it or ignore it.

Power Meters

Power meters have revolutionized cycling training. These devices measure your power output while cycling, giving you an accurate view of your effort.

Power meters are typically installed on the bike's crank, pedals, or rear wheel hub and send data to a compatible device, such as a cycling computer or smartwatch. I have a Quarq Power Meter by SRAM. I can use this power meter with my Garmin Fenix8 smartwatch and Garmin Edge 1050 bike computer. It tells me my watts, cadence, heart rate, and speed while I ride, which helps me adjust and increase my output.

Tracking your performance using a power meter involves monitoring your Functional Threshold Power (FTP). This is the maximum power, measured in watts, that you can sustain for an hour. You can track improvements in your cycling power output by comparing your FTP from various periods.

Cadence Sensors

Cadence sensors measure how often your feet or pedals rotate on a bike in a minute. For runners, an optimal cadence can help improve efficiency and reduce the risk of injury. For cyclists, it can help balance speed and energy expenditure.

Cadence sensors are important. They tell you how many RPMs (or revolutions per minute) you spin. Many people like to stay between 75 and 85 RPM. But sometimes, you may want to spin easily and remain in the mid-90s–100 RPM. Here, you are spinning very fast. (The faster you spin, the more efficient you will become.) Use this when climbing uphill or riding into the wind.

To track progress with a cadence sensor, monitor changes in your average cadence during runs or rides. An increasing cadence could indicate improvements in your efficiency.

Training Peaks/Final Surge/TriDot

Two popular workout tracking systems are on the market today—Training Peaks and Final Surge. There may be others as well. These enable a coach to put in a workout for you and then evaluate the results. You can also do this yourself. If you look at your workouts and have a power meter, you will see these analytics on Training Peaks.

- Work: This is the total energy you use when you work out. It's measured in kilojoules, a fancy way of saying "how much energy you burn." Knowing how hard you worked and how many calories you burned while exercising helps.
- TSS (Training Stress Score): This number shows how challenging your workout was, considering how long and intense it was. You use a single number to show how much strain the exercise puts on your body.
- NP (Normalized Power): Imagine if, instead of your power going up and down during a workout, you could keep it steady the whole time. NP estimates the power you could have kept constant throughout your workout for the same effort. It's used to help figure out your TSS.

- NGP (Normalized Graded Pace): When you're running, this adjusts your pace (how fast you're going) based on whether you're going uphill, downhill, or staying flat and how hard you're working. It gives you a more accurate picture of your effort, considering the changes in terrain.
- Elevation Gain: This is how much you've gone uphill during your workout, measured in feet or meters. It shows you the total height you've climbed.
- Elevation Loss: This is the opposite of elevation gain. It measures how much you've gone downhill, in feet or meters, during your workout.
- Grade: This measures the steepness of the hill you're either going up or down, shown as a percentage. A more significant number means a steeper hill.

Lately, I've been experimenting with TriDot, an AI-generated app. I love how its AI-driven approach creates personalized training plans tailored to my needs. It adjusts based on my progress, pushing me toward the next level with precision and efficiency. This innovative system takes the guesswork out of training and motivates me to improve.

Today's technology provides numerous ways to track your fitness progress. By understanding and effectively using these tools, you can gain deeper insights into your performance, set realistic goals, and track your progress.

As technology advances, you will find bigger and better products than I discussed here. However, data is only valid when acted upon. Use these insights to adjust your training regimen and push yourself toward better performance.

QUICK TIPS

- I've found that the Garmin is the best multisport watch.
- Track your progress. If you dislike using technology, write it on paper or in a notebook. Record every workout and note how you feel.

Ray Cushmore
Triathlete, Rockville Centre, NY

Although I was an athlete in my younger years, playing baseball and running cross country, sports took a back seat after I married and spent two decades as a father.

During this time, I played a little golf, ran an occasional race, and worked on my "dad bod." My kids were active in swimming, starting in local rec leagues and continuing into high school.

Watching my kids swim piqued my interest. Although my first attempt at swimming laps in the pool left my heart beating like a rabbit after only a hundred yards, I gradually worked my way up to longer workouts while also getting back into distance running.

Swimming and running got me thinking about triathlons. However, participating in a triathlon felt intimidating. I didn't know anyone in the sport, and the marketing made it look like all triathletes were superheroes and not for a dad in his mid-50s working his way back into shape.

Encouraged by a friend, I signed up for an indoor triathlon at Lifetime Fitness. It was a nice, safe environment that gave me a taste of the sport and led to registering for my first true triathlon at EventPower LI's Smith Point. Although I had an online training program, there were two significant hurdles: 1) I had no open water experience, and 2) I didn't own a bike.

When I visited a bike store, I was shocked by the $2,000 price tag for "affordable" triathlon bikes. Luckily, another friend offered to lend me his mountain bike, which he had bought at a garage sale. The only issues were that it was too small, the brakes were practically non-existent, and a dog had chewed off part of the seat.

Despite feeling out of place at my first official sprint triathlon at Smith Point, I was determined to avoid making rookie errors (though I can't say the same for future races). The race whizzed by in a blur. I was so caught up in the rush that I lost time. Crossing the finish line was a moment of pure euphoria. Given the circumstances, I placed mid-pack, which made me feel like I belonged.

PART 2

SWIMMING

Practice open water as much as possible. If you can't practice in open water, go to a pool, bring three or four friends, and swim together in one lane to replicate a triathlon. –Gwen Jorgensen

CHAPTER 12

Swimming—The Basics and Gear

"I was doing an aquathlon (run/swim/run). After completing the run and a fast transition, I dove into the water without really looking at the full set of buoys and swam to the wrong buoy. Fortunately, I didn't go around it and swam as fast as I could to the correct buoy, but I added 200 meters to my swim." –Pathetic Triathlete Group Member

Yes, you must know how to swim to compete in a triathlon. I didn't know how to swim when I signed up for my first triathlon in Sanibel, Florida. I had hired a coach who told me to swim 1,600 yards. I couldn't even get across the pool doing a doggy paddle for 25 yards. At that time, I was 53 years old.

He convinced me to join a Masters Swimming team. The swim coach helped me learn how to breathe in the water without throwing up. It wasn't easy, and that's when I realized I needed nose plugs because the water entered my sinuses, making me nauseous and triggering my asthma. In addition to the Masters Swimming team, I also went to the pool at least three to four times a week to practice what I learned. Within weeks, I could easily cross the pool.

Before embarking on hiring a swim coach or signing up for a Masters Swimming program, you should have the basic competency skills as set by the American Red Cross, which are:

- Entering the water–can you comfortably jump in?
- Getting a breath–putting your head under water and taking a breath when you return to the surface.
- Staying afloat–either on your back or front or both.
- Changing position–swim for 5-10 yards and turn around.
- Swimming a distance–swim 25 yards without stopping.
- Getting out of the water safely–pulling yourself out of the water from the pool deck.

If you cannot do one or all of these, I suggest hiring a swim coach to teach you basic skills. Please note that some pools are measured in meters, while others are measured in yards.

Swimming Basics

Although I didn't know how to swim 10 years ago, I do now, and swimming is my strongest discipline. I love it, but it is the most technical of the three. Swimming improves cardiovascular fitness, full-body strength, and flexibility.

Before you get started, you may want to pick up a few items, including:

- Swimsuit
- Goggles
- Swim Cap
- Kickboard
- Fins
- Swim Paddles
- Pull buoy
- Nose plugs (optional)
- Earplugs (optional)

How to Pick a Swimsuit

When I first started swimming for triathlon training, I thought you could wear any swimsuit. I didn't realize that suits produce drag, which makes you slower in the water. I used to buy swimsuits two to three times my size so that no one would see my body fat. But, instead, by purchasing these larger suits, I embarrassed myself even more.

While swimming at Hofstra one day, I noticed people looking at me. When I looked down, I realized why. My left breast was practically out of my suit! So, the story's moral is to buy a bathing suit that is smaller than you need.

Women's cross-back suits feature straps that cross over at the back and are designed to provide tension by distributing weight across your shoulders and reducing pressure points. This can be particularly beneficial for active swimmers.

Typically, women wear a one-piece, tight-fitting swimsuit. Some women like to wear two-piece suits, but I prefer one-piece suits like TYR, ROKA, or BlueSeventy.

When one of my coaches told me to buy a suit three times smaller, I could barely put it on. I struggled to get the suit over my hips. When my coach saw me in it, she said, "Now that one fits you right!" When I told her I couldn't breathe, she explained that bathing suits stretch in the water, which they do.

Men's swim briefs are designed for performance. They reduce drag, provide support, and allow for maximum movement.

Jammers and Tri Kits

Men's jammers are a popular choice among triathletes. They are knee-length swimsuits that offer the same advantages as Speedos but provide more coverage.

Tri kits are another great option. These one-piece suits can be worn for the entire race, eliminating the need to change outfits between disciplines. They come with padding for the cycling segment and are designed to be worn under a wetsuit.

Nose Plugs

Don't feel embarrassed or ashamed if you need to wear nose plugs. Lots of people wear them and swim well with them. For me, it was a game changer. I was getting a lot of water up my nose and was constantly getting sinus infections. The water going up my nose made me gag and dry heave in the pool. Nose plugs eliminated that. By clamping your nose closed, no water goes up it. Once I started using them, I realized I could swim 25 yards easily without stopping. Now, I could swim endlessly with ease, breathing through my mouth.

Try several brands to see which works best for you.

Earplugs

Many people have issues with water entering their ears, which can also cause sinus and ear infections. To avoid this, consider wearing earplugs from the beginning.

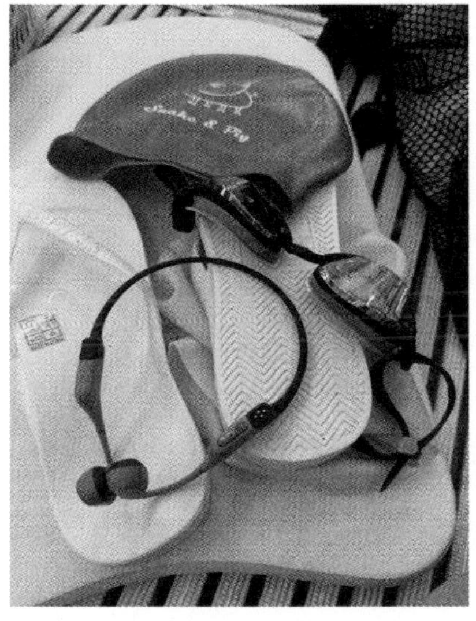

I used to buy children's earplugs that were like Play-Doh. They worked fine, but I wanted something a little less disposable. I found an Ear, Nose, and Throat doctor who made custom earplugs. The custom earplugs are terrific. They fit in your canal and don't come out.

Goggles

It's important to wear comfortable goggles. They should fit snugly around your eyes without leaving red marks. If you're swimming outdoors, consider getting a pair with UV protection.

Try different ones. Every pair is different, and having no water leaks is key. I love the following goggles: Snake & Pig, FORM Goggles, ROKA, FINIS, Speedo, Sable, and TYR. But there are dozens on the market. I know this sounds funny, but you may want to buy a few pairs and check out which works best for you. Some swimming stores, or large athletic shops like Paragon in New York City, have goggles on display, and you can test them out. If you have that opportunity, do that instead of buying several pairs. Put them on your face, and if they don't fall off when you bend your head, they may be the right pair for you.

Swim Cap

A swim cap is another must-have. It reduces drag and keeps hair out of your face. During a race, you must wear a swim cap. So, it's important to get used to it. Plus, it's a great way to show off your personality. Choose a bright color to stand out or a funky design to make a statement.

QUICK TIPS

- Buy the right-fitting (or a smaller) bathing suit.
- Make sure that the goggles fit right. You may need to try various types before finding the one that works best for you and doesn't leak.
- Pools are either yards or meters.

CHAPTER 13

Warm-Ups

"Due to medical issues, I had gained some weight during the offseason. I didn't lose it all before my first wetsuit legal race. My wetsuit was so tight it didn't fill with water during the swim. I struggled to get it off my shoulders. When I got to the wetsuit stripper, she helped me peel it off my arms. I then lay on my back so she could peel it off my legs. It wouldn't budge as she was dragging me through the grass. Finally, another guy held my arms so she could pull it off. That added two minutes to my transition time." –Pathetic Triathlete Group Member

When you first enter the pool, dynamic stretches are a good habit. Dynamic stretching involves active movements that stretch your muscles without holding them. You can do this for up to 10 minutes before jumping in the water.

- Standing Streamline Reach-Ups–Stand straight, interlock your fingers, and extend your arms above your head. Reach upward, then slowly sway from side to side.
- Arm Circles–Extend your arms to the sides and make circles with them, starting small and gradually increasing.
- Leg Swings–Hold on to a wall or rail for support and swing one leg forward and backward. Then, switch to the other leg. This warms up your hips, which are crucial for kick propulsion in all strokes.
- Push-ups–Start in a high plank position, lower your body until your chest touches the floor, and push back up. This warms up your arms, shoulders, and core.
- Jumping Jacks–Stand with your feet together and hands by your sides. Jump up, spreading your legs and swinging your arms to the sides and above your head. Jump again to return to the starting position.
- Cross-Body Arm Swings–Stand tall and swing your arms across your body, alternating.
- Trunk Twists–Stand with your feet hip-width apart and hands on your hips. Twist your torso to the left, then to the right.
- Doorway Pec Stretch–Stand in an open doorway. Place your hands on the door frame, then lean forward to stretch your chest muscles.

QUICK TIPS

- Dynamic stretching aims to warm up your muscles and increase your range of motion, but don't push yourself to the point of pain.
- Always perform these exercises in a controlled manner.

CHAPTER 14

Swim Toys

"At my first Olympic distance tri, I had a panic attack in the water. I flipped onto my back to calm down and swam headfirst into a metal buoy. I blame the head injury on my failure to remember to put my timing chip back on before the bike." –Pathetic Triathlete Group Member

Swim toys, such as fins, a kickboard, paddles, and a pull buoy, are excellent training tools for developing and improving strokes. As a USMS Swim Coach, I suggest buying all these for my athletes.

However, once you buy them, what do you do with them?

Kickboard

A kickboard is a flotation device that swimmers use with their hands. It helps isolate the lower body so swimmers can focus on improving their kick technique and building leg strength. There are so many different types and brands of kickboards on the market today. Get the cheapest one. You don't have to get an expensive kickboard because they all do the same thing. You use them to learn to kick more efficiently. You will use this tool even after you become proficient in swimming.

Try to incorporate a kick workout with every swim workout. Start with a 25-yard kick with the board and work up to 100 yards (four times). I recommend wearing short swim fins and keeping your legs straight by kicking from the hips. I often see swim clients kicking from the knees, which slows them down and is improper form. Also, do not bend your knees. A slight bend is okay, but not a full bend. Your kick should be comparable to a flutter.

There are many benefits of using a kickboard, including:

Technique Improvement

Isolates the Legs—It allows swimmers to concentrate solely on their kicking technique, ensuring they can focus on leg movement without worrying about arm strokes.

Improves Kick Efficiency–By isolating the legs, swimmers can work on the specifics of their kick, such as refining the flutter kick technique for freestyle and backstroke or mastering the dolphin kick used in the butterfly stroke.

Strength and Endurance-Building

Enhances Leg Strength–Regular use of a kickboard can help build muscular strength in the legs, which is essential for powerful starts, turns, and overall propulsion in the water.

Boosts Endurance–Focusing on kicking exercises increases cardiovascular endurance, as it requires sustained effort over extended periods.

Injury Rehabilitation and Prevention

Low-Impact Exercise–For swimmers recovering from upper-body injuries, kickboard drills offer a way to stay in shape and maintain a feel for the water without straining injured areas.

Promotes Proper Alignment–Using a kickboard can help swimmers maintain better body alignment and balance in the water, reducing the risk of injury by promoting efficient movement patterns.

Breathing Control

Breathing Technique–Kickboard drills can also be used to practice and improve breathing techniques. Swimmers can focus on timing and controlling their breath without the added complexity of coordinating arm movements.

You hold the board out and kick. Put your face in the water. Then, when you need a breath, take one on the opposite side to practice bilateral breathing.

Fins

Fins, also called flippers or swim fins, are worn on the feet to improve leg strength, ankle flexibility, body position, and overall speed in the water. They also allow swimmers to focus on their stroke technique without worrying too much about propulsion.

Fins have many benefits, including adding buoyancy and helping to maintain a horizontal position in the water; forcing your legs to work harder, which can improve the strength and efficiency of your kick; feeling more propulsion with each kick, helping to understand the impact of a powerful kick in swimming propulsion; and aiding in increasing the flexibility of your ankles, allowing for a more effective flutter kick.

When you swim, you don't need a long fin. Long fins are typically for snorkeling, while short fins are for swimming. I like FINIS, Aquasphere Fins (my favorite), and Sporti.

A flutter kick drill:

Flutter Kick on Side Drill With Fins

Start Position: Lie on one side in the water, with your lower arm extended above your head and your ear resting on it. Your other arm should rest along your side.

Kick—Flutter kick with the fins. The added resistance and propulsion from the fins will help you maintain a higher speed and improve your feel for the water.

Focus on Technique—Concentrate on keeping your body as straight as possible. Your hips should not drop, and your kick should originate from the hips, not the knees.

Rotation—After a set distance (e.g., 25 meters/yards), switch to the other side to ensure balanced work on both sides of your body. This helps develop symmetry in your kick and overall swimming technique.

Breathing—Practice exhaling underwater and taking quick breaths when you rotate your head. The goal is to keep your movements smooth and your breathing controlled.

Paddles

Swimming paddles, worn on the hands, are super important. They enable you to learn to catch and pull through the water correctly, enhance upper-body strength, and improve stroke technique. They also create more resistance in the water, challenging your muscles and helping you focus on your pulling motion. You can use paddles with any drills outlined in a later chapter, alone, or with fins. I like to start and end the workout using paddles and fins to get into a rhythm.

Pull Buoy

A pull buoy is a flotation device that swimmers place between their thighs. The larger part of the buoy sits on your backside. It helps isolate the upper body, allowing swimmers to focus on their arm stroke and improve their strength. It also helps swimmers maintain proper body alignment in the water. You do not kick with a pull buoy. The pull buoy helps provide endurance and upper-body strength. Plus, it emulates a wetsuit in open water.

QUICK TIPS

- Each of these swim toys will help you become proficient in your stroke.
- Try doing a combination of different drills during each swim set.

Nicole Thomas
Triathlete, Olney, MD

Growing up, I was active but never considered myself athletic. In 2005, as an adult, I discovered cycling and connected with a local group of women through an online message board. It was there that I came across a member discussing a local triathlon. This sparked the thought, "If she can do it, so can I." With encouragement from my partner, Michele, unlike my skeptical parents, I began running in October. I signed up for the Iron Girl Columbia, which comprised a 1000-yard open water swim, a 15-mile hilly bike ride, and a 5K run.

By December, I got into a pool for my first-ever lap swimming session. While I could make it from one end to the other, I knew my technique needed to improve, and I knew that starting with an open-water swimming triathlon was not a good idea.

Opting to shift gears, I made my first race a pool-based triathlon, the 3 Sport Sprint Triathlon, in Richmond, Virginia. This event featured a 400-meter swim, a 12-mile bike ride, and a 5K run. Conveniently, my partner's mother lived in Richmond, making it an ideal location for my first triathlon. To prepare, I started taking swimming lessons that December and persevered with my running despite not feeling entirely confident.

In June 2007, I ran a 5K, my first race of any kind as an adult. I sprained my ankle but finished the race and was very happy with my time. By July, I could barely swim the 400 meters I needed for the triathlon, but I decided to forge ahead with the race.

Caught up in the excitement, I checked out the results from a prior year online. I entertained the possibility of securing a spot on the podium for my age group.

The swim was challenging on race day, but I finished it feeling good. The bike segments went smoothly, but the run proved challenging, leading to an unplanned mix of running and walking. I didn't finish anywhere near the podium. The aftermath disappointed me, and it took me days to come to terms with my performance and appreciate what I had done.

Reflecting on the experience, I realized the significance of completing a triathlon and the importance of celebrating this achievement. My advice to newcomers is to focus on enjoying the journey and to take pride in your accomplishments, regardless of the outcome.

CHAPTER 15

Pool Drills

"The swim leg for my first Olympic distance triathlon was in a bay, and unfortunately, it was windy and wavy. The swim course could not be straighter, an out-and-back course with one turn, but I could not get comfortable swimming in those conditions. I did backstroke for a long time, but the lifeguards constantly had to point me in the right direction. The GPS map of my swim looked like a drunk walking home from an all-night bender." –Pathetic Triathlete Group Member

Swimming in a pool is like learning to play a musical instrument. Just like you practice different scales and chords to get better at music, you do pool drills to improve your swimming.

Pool drills are the ABC of swimming. They help break down swimming into smaller, manageable parts so that you can focus on one thing at a time.

Balance and coordination are important in the water. Certain drills teach you how to control your movements to swim more efficiently.

Just as lifting weights strengthens your muscles, certain drills can make you a stronger swimmer. They can help build the muscles you use for swimming, making you faster and allowing you to swim longer distances without getting tired. Here are some drills:

Fist Drill

A fist drill is important because it encourages you to feel the water from your forearm. It also gives you a high elbow catch in the water and promotes body awareness. Start by taking your hand, making a fist, and swimming.

This drill will help you focus on your core and form. You will feel the difference when you transition to open hand.

Catch-up Drill

In this drill, one arm remains outstretched in front while the other completes an entire stroke cycle. The other arm begins its stroke when the moving arm "catches up" and is outstretched in front.

Importance: The catch-up drill helps improve balance and stroke timing in the water and encourages a long, streamlined position. It also helps you focus on the catch and high elbows in the water. When you enter the water, go wider so that you can make a good catch.

Fingertip Drill

For this drill, as your arm recovers over the water, drag your fingertips lightly across the water's surface until they begin the stroke.

Importance: This drill promotes high elbow recovery.

Single-Arm Drill

This drill involves swimming with one arm while the other stays at your side or outstretched.

Importance: The single-arm drill isolates and focuses on the movements of one arm at a time, allowing you to concentrate on proper technique and feel for the water.

Kick on Side Drill

In this drill, you kick with your body rotated to one side, keeping one arm outstretched in front and the other along your side.

Importance: This drill helps improve body rotation and balance in the water.

Bilateral Breathing Drill

This drill involves breathing on both sides, typically every third stroke. Practice breathing evenly on both sides to develop balance in your stroke and increase oxygen efficiency. The pull buoy lets you focus on your breathing pattern without worrying about leg movements.

Importance: Bilateral breathing promotes balance in the water and ensures you can breathe comfortably no matter which direction the waves are coming from in open-water swims.

Sculling Drill

Sculling involves sweeping your arms back and forth in small movements while keeping your palms flat and fingers spread.

Importance: Sculling drills help you develop a feel for the water and improve your ability to catch and pull water effectively during each stroke.

Core Engagement

This is a drill for enhancing core stability.

With your legs immobilized with a band, focus on engaging your core to keep your body aligned. Rotate your torso from side to side while keeping your legs still. Use your arms and swim as usual without using your legs. This will improve your overall balance and streamline your position.

Arm Stroke Improvement

This is a drill for focusing on upper-body technique. Use a pull buoy. Without kicking, you can concentrate on perfecting your arm strokes, ensuring proper hand entry, and a strong pull-through in the water. This can be done with or without paddles.

Controlled Breathing

This drill develops breathing technique.
Work on exhaling underwater and taking quick, efficient breaths without lifting your head too high, which can disrupt your body position.

Breathing at 3, 5, and 7

Try to breathe every three strokes. This will help with bilateral breathing. Once you have mastered this, try five strokes, then breathe, then seven strokes, and breathe. This will help you get faster, especially in open water.

Resistance Training

This is a drill for increasing upper-body strength.
Combine the pull buoy with hand paddles to increase resistance and strengthen the shoulders, arms, and back muscles. Pull from your lats and reach as far as you can. Try to focus on your lats here.

Longer Sets

This is an endurance-training drill.
To build upper-body endurance, use the pull buoy for longer swim sets or intervals. It isolates the muscles used in swimming and increases the workload.

Active Recovery

This is a recovery and technique-focused drill.
Use the pull buoy for light swimming on recovery days or after intense workouts. This will allow your legs to rest while you work on your technique and maintain your feel for the water.

Initially, swimming can seem daunting and very technical. But you'll see progress quickly with these basics, consistent practice, and patience.

QUICK TIPS

- Swimming training aids like paddles, fins, kickboards, and pull buoys are designed to help swimmers improve their technique, build strength, and increase their efficiency in the water.
- Fins are not cheating. They can make you swim faster and help you improve your kick. However, you are not allowed to wear fins in a race. But for training, they are great.
- Do your drills sometime after you warm up in the water and before the main set. They have a purpose.
- If you are a beginner or feel weak in this area, hit the pool at least three to four times a week.
- If you need extra help or motivation, hire a swim coach or join a Masters swim program.

CHAPTER 16

The Stroke

"The day of the triathlon, the swim was advertised as warm because it was in August. It was not. It took my breath away, and I hyperventilated. I couldn't breathe and spent as much time clinging to a support kayak as I did swimming." –Pathetic Triathlete Group Member

As I mentioned in the previous chapter, swimming is technical. You need to keep your body straight with a tight core. Your legs should be straight. You need to have a high elbow catch in the water. In addition, focus on the glide as if you were a fish. Now, let's break down each part of the stroke.

Body Position

The key to efficient swimming is maintaining a streamlined body position. This reduces drag and makes your movement through the water smoother and faster. Use your core, glutes, and lats to help guide you through the water.

Practice floating drills to get comfortable in the water and understand how your body behaves. Aim for a horizontal position, with your body close to the water's surface. Your head should be neutral, looking downward and slightly forward.

Think about a fish or a dolphin and observe how they move through the water. You can also watch YouTube videos of Katinka Hosszú during the 2016 Olympics or of Michael Phelps. There are many great swimmers; you can emulate them by watching what they do.

Breathing Technique

Proper breathing technique is crucial in swimming. Unlike other sports, breathing in swimming cannot be done at any time; it must be coordinated with your strokes.

Many people like to teach beginners bilateral breathing, which involves breathing from both sides, usually every three strokes. I prefer to breathe out of my right side on every other stroke, but sometimes, you need to breathe bilaterally, especially in open water with waves. So, it's essential to learn how to swim using bilateral breathing and get used to it.

Remember to exhale underwater through your nose or mouth, then inhale quickly when you turn your head to the side. You will get water in your mouth. When you exhale, spit it out before you inhale. Keep one eye under the water while the other is out, and quickly breathe in. Then, with your nose and mouth, blow out into the water.

The Kick

The most common kick in freestyle swimming is the flutter kick. It's a simple and efficient kick that involves small, fast movements originating from the hips. You move your legs up and down quickly to take short flutters. Keep your legs straight and kick from your hips and glutes. Watch this because when many people start, they bend their knees, slowing you down.

Avoid large splashes; they might look powerful, but often mean you're wasting energy. Practice kick drills with a kickboard to isolate and improve your kicking technique.

During these drills, I like using a kickboard with my fins. Otherwise, you feel like you're not going anywhere. However, it doesn't matter how fast you go on these drills. It just teaches you to move through the water.

The Stroke

The front crawl or freestyle stroke is the fastest and most efficient stroke, making it ideal for triathlons. It can be broken down into three phases:

The Catch

Extend your arm forward under the water, palm facing down, elbow slightly bent, and let the tip of your fingers go in first.

The Pull

Draw your hand down and back, under your body, keeping your elbow higher than your hand. Pull the water through almost to the top of your thigh. Think about pulling yourself through the water.

The Recovery

Once your hand reaches your hip, lift your arm out of the water, leading with your elbow. Then, reach as far as you can forward to start the next stroke. While this is done with your arms, your legs perform a flutter kick. Remember to breathe.

QUICK TIPS

When you're in the water, watch out for a few different things:

- The catch—Ensure you have high elbows under the water and follow through by pulling the water to your hip.
- The recovery—Keep your arms straight and shoulder-width apart, keeping them from crossing over your body.
- The kick-Keep those knees straight.
- During a triathlon race, swim freestyle.

Pool Dimensions

- 25-Yard Pool–Common in the US, especially in high schools and recreational facilities.
- 25-Meter Pool–Often used in international competitions.
- 50-Meter Pool (Olympic-Sized)–This pool is used for the Olympics and other major competitive events.

Lengths Required for Common Distances

25-Yard Pool:

- Half Mile–Approximately 36 lengths (0.5 miles = 880 yards)
- Mile–Approximately 70 lengths (1 mile = 1,760 yards)

25-Meter Pool:

- Half Mile–Approximately 32 lengths (0.5 miles = 804.67 meters)
- Mile–Approximately 64 lengths (1 mile = 1,609.34 meters).

50-Meter Pool:

- Half Mile–Approximately 16 lengths (0.5 miles = 804.67 meters)
- Mile–Approximately 32 lengths (1 mile = 1,609.34 meters)

Open-Water Distances

Distance (Miles)	Distance (Yards)
1 Mile	1,760 Yards
2 Miles	3,520 Yards
3 Miles	5,280 Yards
5 Miles	8,800 Yards
10 Miles	17,600 Yards

CHAPTER 17

What to Do at the Pool

"Once, I was training in the pool and decided to dive in. Little did I know it was only four feet deep, and I banged my head on the bottom of the pool. The lifeguards couldn't believe I dove in. I was so embarrassed. I should have seen it was only four feet deep!" –Pathetic Triathlete Group Member

After you purchase your swim toys, bag them up and head to the pool. On the pool deck, complete your dynamic stretches. Focus on warming up for about 10 minutes before getting into the water.

Most swim workouts include a warm-up, drill set, main set, and cool-down.

There are dozens of pool workouts on the internet, the USMS website, and different swim apps, including Swim.com.

As mentioned in chapter 12, pool sizes vary and can be measured in meters or yards. Meters are longer than yards, but the measurements have been used interchangeably for this training manual.

Warm-up

The warm-up should consist of a long, easy freestyle swim. Other strokes are fine to incorporate here. Typically, a warm-up is between 200 and 400 yards (or meters). This is done to warm your muscles and prepare you for the swim workout.

Drills

Incorporate some of the drills mentioned earlier into your workout. I like to do them right after the warm-up, but some swim coaches like to address them after the main set. It's up to you where you want to put them in your workout. (Look at the drill section for drills that suit your needs.) Do approximately 200–400 yards of drills.

Main Set

These can vary depending on the day. Here are some of my favorite distance and speed set workouts.

Distance Sets

These should be done to build your endurance.
I enjoy doing ladders. Here's an example:

Ladder Swim

- 400 yards with fins
- 300 yards with fins and paddles
- 200 yards freestyle swim
- 100 yards kickboard with fins

You can do variations and make them longer or shorter. The thing about swimming is that you need to be consistent. The more consistent you are, the more effective you will be.

Here's another endurance set:

Endurance Set

Main set: 4 × 100 yard freestyle at a moderate pace with a 30-second rest between each 100 yards.

Speed Set

10 × 25 yards fast swims (or you can do 10 × 50 s Fast, or 10 × 100 s Fast). Just so you know, the shorter the interval, the faster you can go. Also, take a 30-second rest between each set.

100 yards easy swim to recover.

Speed Set II

Main set: 8 × 25 yards freestyle sprints with 30 seconds rest between each 25 yards.

Mixed Stroke Workout

Main set: 2 × 100 yards freestyle, 2 × 100 yards backstroke, 2 × 100 yards breaststroke with 20 seconds rest between each 100 yards.

Strength Building

Main set: 4 × 50 yards freestyle with fins and paddles, 20 seconds rest between each 50 yards.

Cool-Down

After your main set, you will do a cool-down. Swim slowly and efficiently for 200 yards to cool down. This is where you will regulate your heart rate and relax your body to end the workout.

QUICK TIPS

- Don't forget to warm up and cool down. Drills should also be incorporated into every workout to build efficiency.
- Use workouts as a guide. If you are just getting started, try these out. Then, build up to 1,200 meters for your sprint triathlon and 2,000 meters for your Olympic triathlon. However, it is a good idea to do more than you can. For example, getting to 2,000 meters for a sprint and 3,500 meters for your Olympic Triathlon won't hurt. This will ultimately help you become a faster and more efficient swimmer.
- Try to break up every workout, and don't do the same one every week. Change it up to develop your skills.

Ahmed Zaher
Triathlete, Coach, Owner of PLAYTRI, Dallas, TX

Growing up, I was always athletic. However, my commitment to fitness dwindled when I pursued a mechanical engineering degree and started working at Mercedes-Benz. My workaholic nature meant that I only managed sporadic gym visits, maybe once a month.

For about a decade, work dominated my life. It wasn't until my divorce that I returned to physical activity, joining a Masters Swimming Program. Several members of this program participated in a triathlon in Louisiana, and they invited me to join as a spectator.

The night before the race, our hotel buzzed with the energy of the triathletes. I was fascinated by their camaraderie and the reverence they showed towards their bikes.

On race day, I was captivated by the sprint. The competitors radiated health and vitality; their beauty lay not in their physical appearances but in their wellness. The diverse range of participants, old, young, big, and small, was inspiring.

At that time, I was a smoker. After witnessing the triathlon, I promised my friends and myself that I would quit smoking and train for a triathlon. That was in August 1999.

By September 1999, I had registered for a race in Dallas. I invested in an affordable aluminum bike and began training. My first triathlon was the Bally's Triathlon, an event I later acquired through my business, PLAYTRI, and renamed the Stonebridge Triathlon.

During the race, I set off fast for the first 100 meters of the swim before switching to breaststroke. I was taken aback by the bike segment as older competitors breezed past me. The transition from the bike to the run, known as a 'brick,' was more challenging than I anticipated, leaving me feeling like I might collapse. I walked for a while before resuming a jogging pace. An elderly man overtook me as if I were stationary, sparking a desire in me to be as fit as him one day.

My love for triathlon has grown immensely since that first race. It led me to compete in Kona 8 times and inspired me to invest my life into the sport. Its impact on my health was transformative, putting me back on track towards wellness.

CHAPTER 18

Swimming in Open Water

"There are no lines or borders when I swim in the open water. I feel free as a fish. However, that's the issue. I feel so free. I forgot to follow the marked buoys." –WeREndurance Member

Open water can produce anxiety and hesitation among triathletes. The ocean's waves can seem daunting, and the current can be strong and forceful. Sometimes, if you are in a significant body of water, you can feel as if the land is so far away, which can produce anxiety.

On the flip side, when you swim in the open water, you feel a sense of freedom that you don't get anywhere else. There are no borders or lines, and there are no restrictions. You can swim wherever and whenever you like.

Anxiety Is Normal

It's normal to feel anxious when swimming in open water. One way to manage this is through controlled breathing exercises. Tread water and take a deep, relaxing breath. Once you feel comfortable, maintain a steady breathing pattern during your swim.

Remember, you can always take a break. It's okay to tread water or float on your back if needed. During a race, you can hold on to the kayak and not get penalized for it.

While swimming in my second race, which was an EventPower LI race in Montauk, Long Island, a racer kicked me so hard that I couldn't catch my breath. I had to hold on to the kayak. After that, the lifeguard told me to count my strokes. I quickly finished because I focused on the strokes, not my fear of being kicked again or my fear of swimming with others so close to me.

Get Used to It

Before mastering open-water swimming, you must get comfortable with the water. Start by acclimating to the water temperature, the feeling of waves, and the absence of pool lines.

If you find a beach, swim within the ropes, if there are ropes. Do that several times before venturing beyond the ropes. Make sure to swim with a friend.

Once you feel comfortable, try swimming in various conditions and bodies of water, such as lakes, rivers, and the ocean. Try to swim in the body of water prior to the race.

Safety Buoy

Make sure to wear a safety buoy when practicing in the open water. This serves a few purposes, including:

- boats and other swimmers can see you
- the pull buoy gives you extra buoyancy so you can hold on to it if you get tired
- you can put water, hydration, and gels in the safety buoy. Most safety buoys have this pocket. It makes it convenient to swim long distances in the open water.

Practice Sighting

Before entering the water, look around. Are there landmarks that you can see while in the water? When I swim at Tobay Beach on Long Island, on one end of the bay, there is a tree resembling a Bonsai tree. I focus on the tree to swim in a relatively straight line.

On the other end, there is a marina. I pick a large boat in the marina as my guide.

As you swim, you will slightly pick your head above the water every few strokes to ensure you're heading in the right direction, staying on course, and not straying off track.

To do this, lift your eyes ever so slightly above the water to look for that landmark or buoy and ensure you swim in the right direction. I like to take 6-10 strokes and look up quickly to make sure I'm going in a straight line.

You can practice this in the pool. During your training sessions, incorporate drills where you lift your goggles from the water every few strokes to see the end of the pool.

In a race, large buoys mark your path. In addition, dozens of people are heading in the same direction. You can follow the crowd, or if you swim faster, swim outside the buoy. However, every race is different. Listen to the directions from the race director.

Drafting

Drafting is legal in open-water swimming and racing. You do this by swimming closely behind another swimmer to take advantage of their slipstream and conserve energy. It's a strategic move in triathlon—practice drafting during your training sessions with a group or in a pool. The key is to stay close, but not too close, to avoid accidental kicking or hitting.

Bilateral Breathing

As mentioned in chapter 15, bilateral breathing helps balance your stroke, allows you to see on both sides, and makes it easier to cope with waves from one direction. Practice bilateral breathing during your pool sessions to make it second nature.

Never Swim Alone

If you go out in the open water, go out with a swimming partner. At the very least, ensure other people are in the water when you enter the water.

Always wear a swim buoy around your waist so boaters and other swimmers can see you.

Be Prepared for the Mass Start

The mass start of a triathlon can be chaotic. Stay calm, start at your own pace, and try to find clear water to swim unobstructed. Safety is paramount. If you're uncomfortable with the mass start, consider starting at the back or the sides of the pack. When I started triathlons, I started at the back and on the side, away from other athletes.

Since mass starts have caused many accidents, many race directors are turning to time trial starts. In these, you start with one or two other people and enter the water together every five seconds, making the entry much safer.

We had a time trial start at the St. Anthony's Triathlon in 2024. Everyone seeded themselves based on how long they could swim, 750 yards. Then, you went out with other people who swam at about the same speed as you. This worked out great. However, it is based on the honor system. Suppose some athletes don't swim as fast as you and enter the wrong corral for whatever reason; this can create a roadblock. Sometimes, it's hard to swim around people, especially if they are swimming the breaststroke, as in St. Petersburg.

Although I seeded myself in the 16-minute category and came in around that time, I could have gone faster if there had been fewer slower swimmers around me.

Where you position yourself at the start can make a big difference. You may want to be at the front to avoid the crowd if you're a strong swimmer. If you need more confidence or are a slower swimmer, consider starting at the back or on the sides. This way, you can avoid much of the initial chaos and swim at your own pace. You can easily pass people who go out too hard when you get closer to the swim exit.

Stay calm. It's easy to get caught up in the adrenaline rush and start too fast, but relax and stick to your planned pace.

Sight Frequently

With all the commotion, it's easy to get off course. To stay on track, check frequently. Look for large, stationary objects that line up with the buoys; they can be easily spotted.

While swimming in the Hudson River during the NYC Triathlon, I went far off course, and the race directors had to veer me back on course. So, keep sighting. It's important.

Simulate race day chaos during training. Practice mass starts with your training group. The more you're used to the hustle and bustle, the less overwhelming it will be on race day. It gets much easier in subsequent races once you've experienced it during a race.

If you become anxious at any point, go back to your drills. To distract yourself from the race, try a catch-up drill. (This always worked for me.)

Open-water swimming is challenging, but with practice and preparation, it can be mastered. The feeling of gliding through the water, with nature surrounding you, is worth every stroke. So, embrace the open water. It's part of the journey that makes our sport unique and rewarding.

Every swimmer is different, so what works for one person may not work for another. Experiment with these tips and strategies during your training to see what works best for you.

QUICK TIPS

- For the first time, go to a place that has a beach and gradually go into the water. Stay by the marked buoys in the beginning before venturing out.
- Practice sighting. This can shave a lot of time off your race.
- Safety is always paramount. Make sure to swim with a buddy and wear a brightly colored swim buoy.

Pool and Open-Water Etiquette

Pool

- Take a quick shower before getting into the pool to help keep the water clean.
- Respect the lane designations—some lanes are for slow, medium, or fast swimmers. Choose the appropriate lane for your speed.
- In shared lanes, swim counterclockwise, keeping to the right side of the lane. This allows multiple swimmers to use the lane efficiently.
- When passing a slower swimmer, do so on the left. Gently tap their foot to ensure they know your approach.
- If you need to rest, move to the corner of the lane to allow others to swim uninterrupted.
- Avoid crowding other swimmers. Leave enough space between yourself and the person in front of you.
- Only dive in designated deep-water areas to avoid injury.
- If you're practicing drills or using equipment like kickboards, pay attention to other swimmers' pace and adjust accordingly.
- Only stop in the middle of the lane if necessary. Finish your lap and then rest.
- Don't wear a bandage to the pool. It will fall off. Be respectful of other swimmers.
- Don't leave your garbage at the pool or in the pool.
- If you wear headphones, be aware that you are not alone in the pool.

Open-Water Etiquette

- Wear a brightly colored swim cap and use a swim buoy for better visibility to boats and other swimmers.
- Be aware of your surroundings. Look for buoys, markers, and other swimmers to avoid collisions.

- Give other swimmers plenty of space to avoid accidental kicks or hits.
- If you're participating in a race or group swim, follow the designated course markers and respect the rules set by the organizers.
- If you encounter trouble, don't hesitate to signal for help by waving one arm and shouting.
- While drafting (swimming closely behind another swimmer) can save energy, always ask for permission during training swims. In races, follow the event's rules regarding drafting.
- Be cautious when entering and exiting the water, especially in rocky or uneven areas. Allow space for others to do the same.
- Always check the weather and water conditions before heading out. Avoid swimming in dangerous situations like strong currents, high waves, or thunderstorms.
- Swim with a buddy or inform someone of your swim plan for added safety.
- Be mindful of marine life, avoid disturbing animals or plants in the water, and don't leave anything that doesn't belong there.
- Again, if you wear headphones, be mindful that other people are swimming around.

CHAPTER 19

Embracing the Wetsuit

"I decided to sign up for Escape from Alcatraz after seeing it on vacation one year. I started training as I'm not a great swimmer and knew the distances for the bike and run. However, in my usual fashion, I didn't fully look at things before signing up. When the videos came out, I watched them. My kids were in another room and heard me talking to myself: "What? The water's 55 degrees? I don't own a wetsuit. Seriously, a shark bite? OMG, that straight-up hill on the run with sand. Did that guy slide out on the bike?" What I heard next were giggles and "Are you ok, Mom?" The following week, I borrowed a friend's wetsuit and tried it on for size at home. No one told me it needed to be wet. Wearing a bra and undies, I got stuck in it, with only my pre-teen son home. He offered to help, but there was no way I could do that to him. Thirty minutes later, it was off."
–Pathetic Triathlete Group Member

Whether you're a seasoned triathlete or just getting started in the sport, one thing is for sure: at some point, you'll need to embrace the wetsuit.

Although wetsuits are not required for triathlons, many use them for buoyancy. Wetsuits are designed to help you float better, reducing your effort and increasing your speed in the water. They also provide insulation, keeping you warm in cooler waters.

The right wetsuit can be a game changer. But with so many options, how do you find one that fits you like a second skin? Wetsuits come in different types, each designed for specific conditions and preferences.

- Shorties–These shorties have short sleeves and short legs, suitable for warm temperatures. I love wearing my BlueSeventy shorties during long summer swims.
- Spring suits–These have no sleeves and long legs. They're perfect for warmer waters, but many triathletes wear them because their arms are not restricted. I love the ROKA Maverick Pro 3 sleeveless wetsuit.
- Full suits cover the entire body, including arms and legs, and are ideal for colder waters. However, many triathletes wear a full wetsuit to streamline and improve their aerodynamics in the water. They are also the fastest suits available. My favorite is ROKA, but another affordable option is the Sumarpo.
- Thermal Wetsuits are perfect for cold-water swimming. With a thermal cap, gloves, and socks, you can swim at 40 degrees Fahrenheit. I also wear a thermal ROKA suit.

Fit Is Important

The most crucial aspect of choosing a wetsuit is the fit. It should be snug but not restrictive, allowing a full range of motion.

All too often, I see people wearing wetsuits that droop at the crotch. However, the suit must be skin-tight, like a life-sized glove. If it's not, it will produce drag, slowing you down. Sizes vary between brands, so refer to the brand's size chart when purchasing.

Put on Chafing Cream

Once you get the right wetsuit, apply chafing cream to key spots, such as your neck, under your arms, groin, ankles, and feet. These areas tend to chafe the most, and this will help prevent that from happening.

Whenever I enter the open water at the beginning of the season, I forget to do this and pay dearly. I get chafed, and it isn't pleasant. I use Aquaphor, but many people use Vaseline or PAM spray. (Yes, the one you use for cooking!) Some people even use lanolin.

Material Matters

Most wetsuits are made from neoprene, a synthetic rubber that provides excellent insulation. However, the thickness of the neoprene varies and is usually denoted by two numbers separated by a slash.

Don't buy a surfer wetsuit or a wetsuit for anything other than swimming.

The first number refers to the thickness in millimeters around the torso (for warmth), and the second refers to the thickness in the limbs (for flexibility). For instance, a 5/3 wetsuit has 5 mm of neoprene in the torso and 3 mm in the limbs. Don't get too caught up in these numbers, but ensure you get the suit you need. Get a thermal suit if you are cold and swim in cold water. Get a full or no-sleeve suit if the water temperature is 65–75 degrees Fahrenheit.

Features

Flexibility—Higher-end suits will have more flexible neoprene in the upper body, allowing for a better range of motion during your swim stroke.

Zipper—Back zippers are standard and typically cheaper, but front zippers provide more accessible entry and exit. When you zip in the back, ensure the pull string is tucked in or looped in the back of the suit.

Seams—Sealed and taped seams provide better water resistance and durability.

Collar—A comfortable collar is crucial to prevent chafing on the neck. Sometimes, collars feel like they are choking you. Make sure to get the wetsuit that fits you right. (Some of my wetsuits are so tight in the neck that I cut them.)

Trying It On

When trying on a wetsuit:

- Wear minimal clothing.
- Slide in one leg at a time, followed by your arms.
- Put gloves on or wear plastic bags on your feet so that you don't tear the suit, and they glide on more easily.
- Pull it up as high as possible before zipping.
- Perform swim motions to test flexibility.

The wetsuit should feel snug (it will loosen up in water) but not restrict breathing or movement.

What to Wear Under Your Wetsuit

Wear a bathing suit or a triathlon kit under your wetsuit. Before a race, I wear my triathlon kit to get used to it in the water and prepare for race day. This way, I will know how transitioning from the swim to the bike feels.

Investing in a wetsuit is important. Take your time, research, try different options, and find the one that feels like it was made just for you.

QUICK TIPS

- Buy a wetsuit that is snug and properly fitting.
- Raise your arms and make sure you don't have resistance, but also make sure it doesn't droop in the crotch.
- Don't forget to put something on your body before entering the open water. This will protect you from chafing.

CHAPTER 20

How to Swim Faster in Open Water

"Last year at multi-sport nationals, there was a swim familiarization time. I had gained weight over the winter, and despite people holding my wetsuit closed, we couldn't get my wetsuit zipped up. I had triathlon shorts on and swam without the wetsuit. It wasn't until I looked at the group pictures we took afterward that I noticed I wasn't wearing a sports bra for the swim." –Pathetic Triathlete Group Member

Open-water swimming is exhilarating yet challenging. Unlike pool swimming, it involves unpredictable elements like currents, waves, and marine life, which lead to slower times than in the pool. However, using the proper techniques and strategies can increase your speed and efficiency in the water.

Improve Your Technique

For starters, keep your body horizontal to reduce drag. Your head should align with your body, looking downward and slightly forward.

For endurance swimming, use a steady, two-beat kick, which means you kick once with each leg for every cycle of arm strokes, creating a rhythm that conserves energy. This helps maintain your rhythm without exhausting your legs. Many people say you should not kick with a wetsuit. However, a two-beat kick has its benefits. It helps maintain a good body position, keeps your rhythm and momentum going, and can assist with steering and stabilization in choppy water conditions. Even with a wetsuit's added buoyancy, a gentle two-beat kick can contribute to overall efficiency without draining energy, making it a strategic choice for longer open-water swims.

Ensure a high elbow catch in the water and a strong pull-through for the arm stroke. This will enhance your propulsion.

Practice bilateral breathing to maintain balance and efficiency in the water. Keep your mouth open slightly and breathe as if you are whistling or playing the flute.

Train for Endurance

Endurance is crucial for open-water swimming. Incorporate long-distance swims into your pool training routine. Interval training, which is periods of high-intensity swimming alternated with rest periods, can also boost your stamina.

Sight Effectively

You must "sight" or lift your eyes above the water to navigate in open water. Practice integrating sighting into your stroke without disrupting your rhythm. Aim to sight once every six to ten strokes.

Draft Smartly

Drafting, or swimming closely behind another swimmer, can save energy and increase speed. Stay close to another swimmer's feet or hip during training to get comfortable with this technique. You will notice bubbles in the water. If you are close, those bubbles will be more prevalent. Stay where you can see those bubbles and practice with a buddy. Take turns, and soon, you will see the benefits of drafting.

Master Your Turns

It's good to practice turning around a buoy. If you don't have a buoy in the open water, practice with an invisible one. Pick a spot and turn around. This will help you on race day.

The other day, I was swimming with my training partner in the open water. I swam around him as he stayed still and treaded water like a buoy. You can have fun with it, but make sure to practice.

Adapt to the Environment

Open water conditions can vary greatly. Train in various bodies of water—lakes, rivers, the ocean—to adapt to different temperatures, currents, and wave patterns.

The following drills will help you get faster in the open water:

Head-Up Swimming (Tarzan Drill)

This drill, suggested by USMS, involves swimming for 10–20 strokes with your head out of the water, looking straight ahead. Swim as you regularly do, but don't put your head in the water. This will help you practice sighting and get used to swimming without seeing the bottom.

Speed Play

This technique, suggested by USA Swimming, involves swimming fast for short periods (10–30 seconds). It's excellent for boosting speed and cardiovascular fitness. After your 10–30-second sprint, recover with a slow, steady freestyle swim for a few minutes and then repeat.

Swim Straight Drill

This drill involves trying to swim as straight as possible. This can be challenging in open water with no pool lines to guide you, but it's crucial for speed and efficiency. Pick a point in the water and try to swim as straight as possible to that point. The point may be a buoy or a landmark you can see in the distance. Try this with a buddy. Have the buddy tread water while you swim 5–10 strokes. Then tread water and see if you align with your swim pal. Alternate with your swim buddy and allow them to swim to you.

Fast-Pace Sets

Swim 50 meters freestyle and complete four sets of 50 meters, alternating between a fast and regular pace. This will improve your speed and endurance.

QUICK TIPS

- Being a good sighter will help your open-water swim.
- When in open water, do intervals.
- Use the drills outlined above to help you pick up speed.

PART 3

BIKING

Try to ride with other people to get the feeling of racing. –Gwen Jorgensen

CHAPTER 21

What You Need to Get Started

"I had a 'new to me' Quintana Roo bike that I had been using for maybe one or two sprint tris. It kept getting flat tires. After taking it to the bike store a million times, I thought it was fixed . . . I went to a sprint tri in southern Missouri. The bike route was a three-loop course. After the swim, I hopped on the bike, and YEP! The back tire was flat AGAIN! I was so pissed; I didn't care if I wrecked the wheel, the tire, or the bike! I did all three loops with a flat tire. Everyone told me I had a flat tire whenever I came around to start the next loop. I gave them a thumbs-up and pedaled as fast as I could! And got nowhere! But I finished!" –Pathetic Triathlete Group Member

Bike riding is not what you remembered as a child when you rode 5 miles per hour on the boardwalk or in a park with your friends. Triathlon training takes bike riding to a new level. You will be riding fast with other cyclists. It's essential to get used to this. Here's what you need to get started:

Helmet

Consider buying a good Multi-Directional Impact Protection System (MIPS) helmet. This safety technology helps protect the brain from angled impacts, making it one of the most critical pieces of gear.

Make sure you try on a few and get the sizing right. I've seen way too many people wear helmets that are too big or too small, which does not protect their heads. If you are unsure about sizing, ask one of the experts at a bike shop. They can help.

Also, helmets only last 3–5 years. Make sure to check the date you purchased the helmet. Over time, helmets degrade and no longer protect your head. Although the helmet may look fine, it is not. So, protect your greatest asset, your head, and get a new helmet every 3–5 years.

Sometimes, the date you buy the helmet and the date the helmet was made could be a year or so apart. Make sure to check the date before you buy. If you can't do that, you may consider returning the helmet to the manufacturer and getting a more current helmet. Then, jot down the date somewhere. And, in the back of your head, make a mental note that you need to replace it in three years. (I recently bought a Giro helmet on sale from the manufacturer. The helmet was dated 2021, but I purchased it in 2024. When I looked it up online, it said that if the helmet was stored correctly, it could last 3 years. So, I kept it.)

Helmets are costly. A good helmet that protects you could cost around $300. Don't skimp here. Your head is precious and needs proper protection.

And please don't use the helmet that has been lying around your garage for the past 10 years. That is not safe.

Eyewear

When you ride, debris from the road will hit your face. Therefore, it is imperative to wear protective eyewear.

I wear prescriptive eyewear and use progressive and transition lenses. It's typically dark out because the transition starts early at a triathlon. However, the sun is high in the sky after the swim, so having those transition lenses is very helpful.

Cycling Jersey

It's nice to have an inexpensive cycling jersey with pockets in the back. You can use those pockets for gels, hydration, or even your iPhone. Many tri kits also have pockets. Training in your tri kit is important to get used to before a race. However, training in cycling jerseys and shorts may be more comfortable for longer rides.

Cycling Shorts/Pants

I also recommend buying cycling shorts and pants, depending on the time of year. These have built-in chamois, which help soften your ride, especially when you go far.

There are different types of chamois. Try on various pairs and find the one that is right for you. If you buy triathlon shorts, the chamois will be minimal and won't give you the padding you would get from cycling shorts or pants. Many people say that typical cycling shorts should not be worn to a triathlon because the chamois are oversized and may fill up with water, creating a diaper effect. However, I have worn cycling shorts instead of tri shorts in some triathlons, which have worked perfectly.

Socks or No Socks

Socks are a preference. I wear wool socks in the winter. In the summer, I either go sockless with my cycling shoes or wear a thin pair of socks.

Cycling Shoes

Cycling shoes are not made for walking. During a triathlon, you must run in these shoes as you transition from the bike to the run. They are a vital part of your cycling gear. If it's your first triathlon, you can wear sneakers. If you get into cycling, you will want cycling shoes because they make pedaling much more efficient. The shoes enable you to not only push down but also pull up.

Another factor to consider is that there are many different brands of cycling shoes. Once you buy a pair, you will have it for years to come. Try on different brands and find one that fits your feet. I like the PEARL iZUMi, Specialized and Santic cycling shoes.

Optional: Gloves

I like to wear fingerless gloves in the summer and real gloves or mittens in the winter to protect my hands. Fingerless gloves are helpful because they allow you to lean on the bike, prevent calluses, and make the ride more comfortable. They also protect you if you fall. Gloves or mittens are important in the winter, as your hands will get cold.

Hydration

Hydration is crucial when cycling because it helps maintain energy levels, regulates body temperature, and prevents dehydration. Dehydration can lead to decreased performance, muscle cramps, and even more serious health issues. While on the bike, you should aim to drink about one bottle (16–20 ounces) of water per hour, adjusting for factors like heat, humidity, and intensity of the ride. Staying hydrated keeps you strong and focused, allowing you to perform at your best throughout your ride.

Hydrating properly will set you up for your run off the bike. Make sure to keep hydrating on the bike. With my road bike, I have two cages where I put two 20–24 ounces of liquid hydration with calories and protein to keep me going. I have an aero bottle for my tri bike that sits between my aero bars, and I can drink from it anytime. Sometimes, I use a CamelBak, Ultimate Direction, or a Drankful backpack or fanny pack while on the bike so that I don't have to grab the water bottles, as there have been times the water bottle has dropped from my hand or the cage.

QUICK TIPS

- Get yourself a MIPS helmet. Don't skimp here.
- Cycling shorts or pants with chamois inside make for a much more comfortable ride.
- Make sure to stay hydrated so that when you run after the bike portion, you are prepared.

CHAPTER 22

Choosing the Right Bike

"On my first ever triathlon, I didn't notice I had lost one of the lenses of my sunglasses. I have all my bike and run pictures dressed up like pirates." –Pathetic Triathlete Group Member

If this is your first race, you don't need to buy a new bike. You can compete in a triathlon on any bike. A friend did his first triathlon on a cumbersome mountain bike. But once he knew he would participate more often, he bought himself a good used bike.

If you have a hybrid or mountain bike and want to try a triathlon, go for it. But you will be at a disadvantage. You will go slower than riding a road or triathlon bike. The bike you train and race on can significantly impact your performance, comfort, and overall enjoyment of the sport.

Types of Bikes

Road bikes are versatile and great for various kinds of riding, from leisure to races. They have a lightweight design, thin tires for less rolling resistance, and drop handlebars allowing multiple hand positions. A road bike is often a good choice for beginners because it balances speed, comfort, and cost.

My first bike for a triathlon was a road bike. I purchased it from a local bike store when I signed up for my first triathlon. I chose a Trek bike because I had heard of the brand but didn't know much about it.

Many excellent road bikes are available, including Felt, Specialized, Argon 18, Cannondale, Quintana Roo, and Cervelo.

Triathlon-specific bikes, known as time trial bikes, are designed for speed. They have aerodynamic features, such as a forward seat position, flat handlebars, and aero bars. These features allow for a more aggressive, aerodynamic riding position, which can help save energy and increase speed.

I asked Ahmed Zaher of PLAYTRI in Dallas, Texas, what he thought was the most important aspect of buying a new bike. He said, "A bike that is easy to adjust for fitting. Athletes change over time, and you want one bike that can fit them perfectly regardless of their goals and progress."

Components

There are two popular bike component brands–Shimano and SRAM–but other brands are breaking through, including Campagnolo. Since Shimano and SRAM are the most popular at the time of publication, I will focus on them in the following chapter.

Brakes

SRAM brakes are generally perceived as softer and spongier, offering a more gradual braking feel. On the other hand, some riders find Shimano brakes lock up fast, providing a more immediate stop. The preference between these two types of braking responses largely depends on individual riding style and comfort.

Drivetrains

The drivetrain on a bike refers to the components that deliver power from the rider's legs to the bicycle, enabling it to move. SRAM drivetrains are often praised for their crisp and clean shifting, while Shimano drivetrains are known for their durability and reliability.

Bike Fit

Getting the right fit is essential, no matter which bike you choose. An incorrect bike fit can lead to discomfort and injury. Many bike shops offer professional fitting services. During a bike fitting, height, flexibility, and riding style are considered to adjust the saddle height, saddle position, handlebar height, and reach. It's a worthwhile investment that can enhance your comfort and performance.

I asked Mike Monastero, triathlon coach and owner of Babylon Bike Shop in Babylon, NY, what he thought. Mike has been fitting my bikes for years and has an excellent eye for fit, and this is what he had to say:

> An athlete's bike fit is all about how comfortably and safely they can ride their bike during training and events while staying aerodynamic for a fast transition to running. A cheaper bike that fits well, allowing the rider to stay in an aero position and produce their best power, is better than an expensive, poorly fitting bike that causes discomfort and forces them to sit up often. Athletes should seek recommendations from their local triathlon community for fitters who have successfully fitted triathletes of all shapes, sizes, and levels. A good fitter will watch you pedal, aiming for balanced body use and a strong, controlled pedal stroke. They should adjust the bike to you, not make you adapt to it. Discomfort shouldn't be ignored or accepted as normal. A rider's body changes over time with training, so bike fits may need to be updated to stay comfortable and efficient.

Test Ride

Before purchasing, if you can, test-ride a few bikes. Some shops don't allow you to do this, especially with a triathlon bike. However, if possible, it will help you compare how different models feel and handle the road. Pay attention to the bike's weight, how comfortable you are in the saddle, how easily you can reach the handlebars, and how smoothly the bike shifts gears.

New vs. Used

Buying a used bike can be a good option if you're on a tight budget. However, it's important to have a knowledgeable person or a trusted bike shop check it over for potential issues. A cheap bike that doesn't fit you or needs constant repairs can cost more in the long run than investing in a quality new bike.

My training partner bought a used Giant bike nearly five years ago and still rides it today.

Mike had a lot to say about new versus used bikes as well.

> Both options have advantages when deciding between buying a new or used bike. Your bike is the most significant expense in triathlon, and a good purchase can significantly enhance performance. Many athletes consider used bikes from reputable companies like Trek's Redbarn Refresh, The Pros Closet, and Bicycle Blue Book. These businesses often offer bikes with modern features at a lower cost than new ones, and they inspect and certify the bikes, ensuring safety and legitimacy.
>
> However, buying used may require additional spending to achieve the optimal fit, such as changing the saddle, stem, aero bars, or gearing. This can diminish the initial savings. Used bikes also typically lack warranties. Buying new, on the other hand, includes a manufacturer's warranty and potentially service support from retail stores, which can offer fittings to customize your bike to your needs. For these reasons, some athletes might prefer the peace of mind of purchasing a new bike.

QUICK TIPS

- Choosing the right bike involves considering your budget and the type of bike that suits your needs, ensuring the correct fit, and taking potential bikes for a test ride.
- Determine whether buying a used bike or investing in a new one works for you. The bike is the most expensive part of triathlon training, but once you have the right one, you will have it for years.
- Don't forget the chamois cream. You don't want to get saddle sores!

A Word About Saddle Sores . . .

Chamois cream is crucial in providing comfort and preventing discomfort during cycling. It is a specially formulated cream that reduces friction between your skin and clothing, preventing the painful condition known as saddle sores. Saddle sores are skin ailments experienced by cyclists due to extended periods spent on a bike saddle. These can range from simple skin irritations to abscesses or boils caused by the constant rubbing, pressure, and sweating.

By using chamois cream, cyclists can reduce their risk of developing these sores, ensuring a more comfortable and enjoyable riding experience. I use Zealios' Betwixt and have been using it for years. You may like this brand or find another one that works well for you.

CHAPTER 23

Understanding Your Bike's Components

"At the USA Triathlon Multisport Festival, my bike derailleur exploded and broke on the first downhill. I ended up walking my bike the entire bike course. I finished, but the experience taught me a thing or two about not giving up!" –Pathetic Triathlete Group Member

To optimize your cycling performance, it's essential to understand the various components of your bike. Each part is crucial in how your bike functions and can affect your ride.

Frame

The frame is the backbone and biggest component of your bike. It holds all the other parts together. Frames can be made from various materials, including aluminum, steel, carbon fiber, and titanium. Each material has its strengths and weaknesses regarding weight, strength, ride quality, and cost. I purchased carbon fiber road and tri bikes because of their lightness. Do your homework and find out which material would be right for you.

Wheels

Your bike's wheels significantly impact its performance. Lighter wheels can improve your bike's acceleration and climbing ability. When you buy a new or a used bike, it will come with wheels. However, you can easily upgrade them. A good retailer will help you find the right wheels for you. But I also encourage you to do your homework. Find out what the reviews are saying and go to the retailer with an idea of what you want.

Tires

Tires provide traction and absorb shock. According to the research, wider tires are better because they have lower resistance than narrower tires, which makes them faster. However, it's important to note that riding surfaces are imperfect. So, you must correct your tire pressure depending on the tire width.

I purchased tubeless tires for my tri bike so that if I ride long and get a flat tire, I don't have to change it. The tire will automatically inflate to fill the hole. However, they leak, and sometimes, I have difficulty pumping my tires because they easily get clogged up. So, there is a trade-off.

Drivetrain

The drivetrain includes all the parts that transmit power from your legs to the wheels:

- Crankset–This is the component to which your pedals attach. It includes one or more chainrings (the big sprockets).
- Cassette–This is the set of sprockets on the rear wheel.
- Chain–The chain connects the front chainring(s) with the rear cassette, transferring power from the crankset to the rear wheel.
- Derailleurs–These devices move the chain from one gear to another when you shift.
- Shifters–These controls are on the handlebars and allow you to change gears. (When you buy a high-end road or tri bike, you can get Di2 shifters, which are electronic shifters.)

Brakes

Many road bikes feature caliper brakes that squeeze brake pads against the wheel's rim to slow down or stop. These brakes are lighter, cheaper, and simpler to maintain; however, they are less effective in wet conditions and wear out over time. Some models have disc brakes, which provide more consistent stopping power, especially in wet conditions. Disc brakes are powerful and consistent in all conditions, but they are expensive to add on.

Saddle

The bike saddle, or seat, is where you sit. A good saddle should support your sit bones. It may be appropriately padded and suit your anatomy to ensure comfort during long rides.

Handlebars

Triathlon bikes usually have aero bars, which are handlebars with extensions that allow you to rest your elbows and ride in a more aerodynamic position. This can significantly improve speed and efficiency over long distances.

Many people who have road bikes ask me if they should get aero bars for their road bikes. It may make sense if you are always on a long, flat road. Or, if you are a beginner and want to experience what it feels like to have aero bars. However, they are not good for group rides because of the handling issues. If you are starting out, you're better off buying a road bike. It's much more versatile.

Pedals

Pedals come in different styles. Some are flat, suitable for casual riding with any shoes. Others, called clipless pedals, connect to special cycling shoes to improve pedaling efficiency.
I like to ride with "lollipop" clips, which SPEEDPLAY makes. These pedals look like lollipops, while many other brands, including Garmin and Shimano, look more like traditional bike pedals.
When I started, I bought pedals with clips on one side and a flatbed on the other, so I didn't have to wear cycling shoes if I didn't want to.

QUICK TIPS

- Know before you buy. Do your research and be knowledgeable to ask the salesperson informed questions.
- Make sure the seat and fit are suitable for your riding ability.
- Check out the different pedals and see which ones are right for you.
- Get a professional bike fit.

Should You Buy a Road or Tri Bike?

I recommend starting with a road bike if someone is new to triathlon. Here's why.

- Road bikes are more versatile and can be used for triathlons, group rides, casual cycling, and other cycling events.
- They are easier to handle, especially for beginners unaccustomed to riding in various conditions.
- The more upright position of a road bike tends to be more comfortable for longer training rides and helps build confidence and skills.
- Road bikes offer better access to brakes and more control over handling, which is crucial when riding close to other cyclists or navigating turns and stops.
- Once you have gained experience and are focused on improving your performance, consider investing in a triathlon bike.

CHAPTER 24

Basic Bike Maintenance

"During a recent aqua bike race, I finished the bike portion, racked my bike, took off my bike shoes, and put on running shoes, but never took off my bike helmet. I ran across the finish line wearing my bike helmet."
–Pathetic Triathlete Group Member

Knowing basic maintenance skills is essential to keeping your bike in top condition. Ensuring you are equipped for safety is vital for any triathlete. It enhances your performance and ensures your bike is safe during training rides and race day.

Changing a Flat Tire

Every cyclist must know how to change a flat tire, and there are lots of YouTube videos that can help. But here are step-by-step instructions:

1. Remove the wheel from your bike.
2. Use a tire lever to pry the tire off the rubber rim.
3. Pull out the inner tube, then check the inside of the tire for sharp objects. Look at the outside of the tire to ensure no objects are sticking out.
4. Inflate the new tube slightly, then tuck it inside the tire.
5. Fit one side of the tire onto the rim, then fit the other. Be careful not to pinch the tube. If you do so, you can get another flat.
6. Inflate the tire to the correct pressure. It's a good idea to have a CO_2 cartridge and inflator on every ride.

Cleaning the Chain

A dirty chain can wear out faster and compromise your bike's performance. Clean it regularly using a chain cleaning tool or a brush and soapy water, then dry it and apply a suitable bicycle chain lubricant. I like to use a rag and wipe off the excess grime from the chain. Then, spray it with a chain lubricant and wipe it again.

Adjusting Brakes

If your brakes are too loose or too tight, they won't work effectively. Locate the brake cable bolt on your bike's brake calipers to adjust them. Loosen this bolt, adjust the cable's tension, and then tighten the bolt again. Your brakes should be tight enough to stop your bike quickly. If you have disc brakes, you may want to let the bike store handle this. You will need special tools. YouTube is your friend. Make sure to do your homework before attempting it on your own.

Safety Equipment

Lights

You will need lights if you ride in low-light conditions or the dark. The standard setup is a white light at the front and a red light at the back. Today, many lights are rechargeable and easily mounted on your bike.

I often ride when it's dark and then at first light. In those situations, I want lots of lights on my bike and even have one attached to my helmet.

Reflective Gear

Reflective clothing or accessories increase your visibility to others on the road. This can include vests, ankle bands, or even reflective stickers on your helmet or bike.

My riding partner and I often shake our heads when it's dark out, and the person riding toward us is wearing all black with no lights or reflective gear. Even if you have lights, it's important to wear something reflective to be seen by motorists and other cyclists.

Make sure to practice defensive cycling. There are a lot of riders out there who think they own the road. They are in the zone, and they are riding 20+ mph. If you're not riding that fast, let them pass. Don't "hog" up the road. But if you are the one riding faster than 20+ mph, be alert and defensive. Look around you. Slow down when you get to an intersection, and be aware.

Communicate

Use hand signals to indicate turns, slowing down, or stopping. Make eye contact with drivers to ensure they've seen you. Here are some hand signals that you should use on the road:

- Slow Down—To indicate slowing down, most cyclists extend their left arm (right arm for those cycling in the UK) out to the side and wave their hand up and down at the wrist.
- Stop—To signal a stop, extend your left arm to the side with the palm facing backward. This is universally recognized as a sign that a cyclist is about to stop.
- Left Turn—Before you slow down for a left turn, extend your left arm straight out to the left, parallel to the ground.
- Right Turn—It is common to signal a right turn by extending your right arm straight out.
- Hazard—If a road hazard, such as a pothole or debris, is present, cyclists often point to it so those behind them can avoid it.
- Changing Lanes—If you're changing lanes or need to move within a lane, it's helpful to signal this. You can do this by extending your arm and pointing in the direction you're about to move.
- Ride Defensively—Assume that others may not see you and be prepared to take evasive action.
- Plan Your Route—Choose routes with less traffic and slower speeds if possible. Bike lanes and paths are preferred. Various apps, including Plotaroute, Ride with GPS, and MapMyRide, have bike routes.

QUICK TIPS

- Wear bright or neon colors when you ride, especially on the road, to increase visibility.
- Practice defensive cycling. Don't assume that drivers see you.
- Use hand signals and ensure the people behind you know what you are doing.

Adina O'Neill
Head Triathlon and Swim Coach, Team B*Real, Milton, MA

My initiation into the world of triathlons began with just the swimming portion. My friend, who was training for a triathlon, was apprehensive about swimming, especially in the ocean. Having spent my entire life swimming in the ocean, I volunteered to do it for her despite never having competed in a swimming event. In addition, I didn't swim much when my children were young.

I started training in the local pool and rented a wetsuit for the event. When I emerged from the water on race day, I was exhilarated, thinking it was the most exciting thing I'd ever done.

My brother, an accomplished triathlete with 11 Ironman events under his belt, and my children, both participants in a "kids" triathlon, were huge inspirations. Watching them compete was thrilling.

Then, my friend invited me to participate in a 5K run, something I had never done before. After some training, I completed the run in 32 minutes, impressing myself and prompting my kids to suggest that I attempt a triathlon.

Taking their advice, I bought a bike and started comprehensive training, swimming, biking, and running. I registered for the Fantastic Nantasket Triathlon in Hull, Massachusetts. The race included a quarter-mile swim, a 15-mile bike ride, and a 5K run. I participated in this event, which took place in the rain the day before my 41st birthday.

Having already experienced the swim, I felt comfortable with it. However, coordinating all three segments was challenging. My brother offered valuable tips, but I needed more specialized gear.

Under my wetsuit, I wore a regular sports bra and spandex shorts, not cycling shorts. After the swim, I felt good and confidently ran into the transition area. I planned to consume an energy gel immediately after.

I felt great on my bike, especially as the rain had eased off. There were a few hills, but I had practiced them during training.

The run was my biggest hurdle. Conducted on the beach, I managed to maintain my pace from the bike ride, alternating between running for nine minutes and walking for one. I remember thinking how surreal the whole experience was.

Crossing the finish line was an overwhelming moment of triumph. "I did it!" I thought. My father, who had come to support me, was at the finish line. The weather had deterred the rest of my family from coming, but having him there made it special. My friend was also there, and seeing them both filled me with joy.

The sense of accomplishment and the electrifying atmosphere made the entire experience unforgettable.

CHAPTER 25

Bike Handling Skills

"At a triathlon I did, the bike course was described as rolling hills. It was rolling over small mountains. When I finished, I spent more time walking my bike up hills than riding and had an average speed of 10mph. To make matters worse, a kid doing his first tri stopped me to ask how to use the Apple Watch for subsequent events, and it distracted me to the point that I forgot to take my electrolytes and energy chews, so of course, I bonked on the bike." –Pathetic Triathlete Group Member

Learning good bike handling skills is essential. All races are different, so you must have good bike handling skills. You will need to know how and when to shift gears, climb hills, descend hills, and cornering. Keep practicing. By doing so, you can handle any situation.

Shifting Gears

When I first started preparing to compete in a triathlon, shifting was new to me. Learning to shift is essential because it will make your ride smoother and more efficient. Try different gears on a flat road to get used to shifting. Then, when you climb hills, you will know how to manage them.

Climbing Hills

Change your gears before you need them. Shift to an easier gear before climbing a hill, not halfway up when you're struggling to pedal. You may put too much pressure on the tires, causing the chain to slip, which happened to me during the Mighty Hampton Triathlon. As I was going uphill, I tried to shift gears quickly and not lighten the pedals, and my chain dropped.

Riding at the Alpha Win Hudson Valley Triathlon. Saugerties, NY.

Here are some tips for climbing hills:

- Shift into an easier gear as you approach the hill to maintain your cadence.
- Rather than attacking the entire hill, maintain a steady, sustainable effort.
- Standing up on the pedals can help on steeper sections, but also uses more energy. Use this technique sparingly. If you can't stand up on a bike, don't try it. (I don't stand on the bike.)

Descending

Keep your weight back. This provides stability and prevents you from crossing the handlebars if you need to stop suddenly. Use both brakes, but use the rear one slightly more. Finally, look where you want to go, not directly in front of your bike.

Cornering

Good cornering technique allows you to maintain speed and control. Here's how:

1. Slow Down Before the Corner–It's safer and more efficient to slow down before you reach the corner and then accelerate out of it. This was my problem when I was turning the corner at a recent triathlon and skidded out.
2. Look Through the Turn–Your bike will naturally follow your gaze, so look where you want to go.
3. Lean the Bike, Not Your Body–Keep your body centered over the bike and lean it into the turn.

Different weather conditions and terrains can present unique challenges. Here's what to consider:

- Wet roads can be slippery. Slow down, especially on corners. Avoid painted road markings and metal surfaces like manhole covers, as they can be particularly slick when wet.

Handling different weather conditions and terrains.

- If you're riding in a storm, keep a firm grip on the handlebars, stay low to reduce resistance, and be ready for sudden gusts.
- Use your gears as much as possible. That is what they are there for. Try practicing on different routes and roads to prepare for your upcoming race.

QUICK TIPS

- Make sure to try riding in different conditions. The more you learn to handle them, the better equipped you will be on race day.
- Try different routes with hills, sharp corners, etc. This will help you determine how to handle yourself during a race.

Etiquette Tips for Safe and Respectful Cycling

- Always wear bright and reflective clothing, especially on foggy days or during twilight and dawn. This helps you stay visible to motorists and other cyclists.
- If you pass someone, always pass on the left side (or the right side if you cycle in the UK) and shout, "On your left." This alerts the person ahead of you and prevents accidents.
- Always wear a bike helmet. It's the most critical safety gear to protect you in an accident.
- Give a wave, nod, or even a friendly quack hand gesture to the person passing you on the other side. It's a courteous way to acknowledge fellow cyclists.
- Use hand signals to indicate turns and stops. This helps communicate your intentions to other cyclists and motorists.
- Follow all traffic signals and signs. Stop at red lights and stop signs, and yield to pedestrians.
- Watch for obstacles, such as potholes, debris, and pedestrians. Always be aware of your surroundings.
- Keep a safe distance from other cyclists and vehicles. This will give you more time to react if the person before you stops suddenly.
- When riding in a group, ride single file in narrow or high-traffic areas to allow cars to pass safely.
- If you're leading a group ride, point out hazards like gravel, glass, or parked cars to those behind you.
- Avoid sudden movements or swerving. Ride predictably so others know what to expect.
- Use front and rear lights when riding in low-light conditions. This increases your visibility to others.

- Regularly check your bike's brakes, tires, and chain to ensure everything works before heading out.
- If you wear headphones or earbuds, ensure you can hear the outside world. Someone may be calling you, and you won't hear if the music is too loud. Avoid any dangerous situations by hearing everything around you. (I like to wear Shokz headphones. They are bone conductor speakers, so I can hear the world around me.)

CHAPTER 26

How to Ride Faster

"I competed in a local triathlon and saw an athlete on a superbike riding very seriously with his helmet backward on his head." –Pathetic Triathlete Group Member

When I first started training for triathlons, my coach told me to spin the wheels at 90 RPMs. So, I did. Instead of picking up speed, I went 5 miles an hour and felt like I would fall off the bike. It wasn't until a few years later that it started to click, and I began to understand why intervals were so important.

You must consistently incorporate interval training, hill repeats, and long, steady Zone 1 (slow, easy rides) to ride faster. Here are some workouts you can use during your training.

Interval Sprints

This workout greatly increases your power output and speed, particularly for sprint triathlons.

Warm-up: 15 minutes of easy cycling, keeping your heart rate low or in Z1.

Main set: 8 repetitions at 30-second all-out sprints with 90 second rest between each sprint. This may be hard, but the more you do these, the easier they become, and you will ride faster.

Cool-down: 15 minutes of easy cycling.

Hill Repeats

Hill repeats help build strength and power, benefiting sprint and Olympic-distance triathlons. You can find a hilly course and ride it. If you can't access a hilly course, try to find one that's at least a quarter of a mile high. Then, you can do this workout.

Warm-up: 15 minutes of easy cycling.

Main set: 5 × 3-minute uphill efforts at a hard but sustainable pace, with 3 minutes of easy cycling downhill between efforts

Cool-down: 15 minutes of easy cycling.

Long Steady Distance

This workout helps build endurance, which is particularly important for Olympic-distance triathlons. You ride here at a moderate level, meaning it's not too hard but not too easy. Keep your cadence at 75–85 RPM and keep the pace steady with your heart rate in Zone 1 and Zone 2.

Ride for 60–90 minutes at a steady, moderate level.

Tempo Rides

Tempo rides are done at a "comfortably hard" pace, a Z3 (also called a sweet spot), and can help improve your lactate threshold, which is crucial for both sprint and Olympic-distance triathlons.

Warm-up: 15 minutes of easy cycling.

Main set: 20 minutes at a challenging but sustainable pace.

Cool-down: 15 minutes of easy cycling.

Fartlek Workout

Fartlek workouts involve varying your pace throughout your ride, which can help improve your speed and power.

Warm-up: 15 minutes of easy cycling.

Main set: 45 minutes of mixed-intensity riding (vary between easy, moderate, and hard efforts).

Cool-down: 15 minutes of easy cycling.

Here Is a 2-Week Sample Bike Workout Plan

Please refer back to Understanding Training Zones, chapter 10.

	Tuesday	Thursday	Saturday
Week 1	Ride hills	Tempo ride	Ride easy for 1 hour
Week 2	Fartlek ride	Easy ride for 45 minutes at an easy Z1 pace	Ride for 1.5 hours in Z1

QUICK TIPS

- Incorporate all these workouts into your training program. Mix it up. Don't do the same one all the time. Try a different type of workout every week. This will help you get stronger and faster on the bike.
- Every weekend, allocate one day to ride your long rides. I like to ride long on Saturdays.

CHAPTER 27

Embracing the Indoor Trainer

"I borrowed a friend's bike for my race since it was much nicer, and I didn't realize there was a gearshift, so I stayed in the same gear the entire race." –Pathetic Triathlete Group Member

As a newbie, you may or may not have access to an indoor trainer, a device that lets you ride your bicycle stationary indoors. It works by holding your bike in place while allowing the rear wheel to turn freely against resistance. This resistance can be adjusted to simulate different riding conditions, like going uphill or riding on flat ground. It's like bringing your outdoor cycling experience indoors so you can train, exercise, or ride for fun, regardless of the weather or time of day.

My first trainer was a CompuTrainer. It worked great and never broke down, but after about ten years, I wanted something with fewer wires. So, I researched and decided to buy the Zwift Hub. Many triathletes have the Wahoo KICKR or a different Wahoo product.

Over the years, indoor trainers have evolved significantly. While CompuTrainer was once considered the *crème de la crème* of indoor trainers, newer models like the Wahoo KICKR have taken the lead with their advanced features and superior user experience.

However, you don't need an indoor trainer to ride indoors. If you can access a gym, you can ride on a stationary bike when the weather is inclement.

What to Look for When Buying an Indoor Trainer

Several types include direct drive, wheel-on, and smart trainers. Direct drive trainers provide the most realistic experience but are usually more expensive. Wheel-on trainers are less costly and easier to use. Smart trainers can adjust resistance automatically and often come with built-in sensors.

Direct Drive Trainer

You remove your bike's rear wheel and connect it directly to the trainer.

The bike's chain drives a cassette attached to the trainer's resistance unit. The pros are:

- More accurate power measurement.
- More realistic road feel.
- Quieter operation compared with wheel-on trainers.
- Eliminates tire wear since the rear wheel is removed.

The cons are:

- They are more expensive than wheel-on trainers.
- Heavier and less portable.

Wheel-On Trainers

With wheel-on trainers, you keep the rear wheel on your bike. The bike stands on the trainer, and the rear wheel rests against a resistance unit. You secure the bike onto the trainer using a clamp on the rear axle. They are more affordable than direct drive trainers, easier to set up, and portable. The negatives include wear and tear on the rear tire, noisier than direct drive trainers, less accurate power measurement, and feeling less like riding on the road.

Smart Trainers

Smart trainers can be either direct drive or wheel-on, but are distinguished by their ability to wirelessly connect to external devices (such as smartphones, tablets, or computers) via technologies such as Bluetooth or ANT+. This connectivity allows them to automatically control resistance based on a virtual riding environment or training program.

Here are the pros:

- Interactive training sessions with apps like Zwift, TrainerRoad, etc.
- Automatically adjust the resistance to simulate real-world conditions, such as hills.
- Track and record a wide range of data for training analysis.

The cons include:

- More expensive than basic (non-smart) trainers.
- Require a compatible device and possibly a subscription to a training app.

Price

Indoor trainers can range from a few hundred dollars to over a thousand. Determine your budget beforehand.

Connecting Indoor Trainers to Your Computer

Indoor trainers connect to your computer or smart device using Bluetooth or ANT+ wireless technology. This enables real-time tracking of your performance data, such as speed, power, and cadence. It also allows you to ride in virtual environments and compete with other cyclists worldwide.

Online Programs

Once you buy an indoor trainer, consider which program you want to use. Zwift is an online cycling and running platform that enables users to interact, train, and compete in a virtual world. In Zwift, your bike's resistance adjusts according to the virtual terrain you're riding, simulating real-world riding. TrainerRoad, on the other hand, focuses on structured workouts and training plans. It provides power-based training with a vast library of workouts and plans.

Zwift and TrainerRoad can be used simultaneously, allowing users to benefit from structured workouts while enjoying Zwift's immersive environment.

There are other training apps on the market that also interact with your indoor trainer. I've heard Rouvy is a good app, but I haven't tried it yet.

Riding in a Virtual World: The Zwift Experience

Riding in Zwift's virtual world is an engaging experience. You can ride courses inspired by real-world locations and participate in races or group rides. Interacting with other riders adds a social element that makes indoor training more enjoyable.

What Are Cadence Sensors and Power Meters?

A cadence sensor measures how fast you're pedaling in terms of RPM. Think of tracking how quickly your legs turn in circles while you pedal. This device can be attached to your bike's crank arm (the part connecting the pedal to the bike) or the bike's frame near the pedals. Here's why it's useful:

- Knowing your cadence helps you train more efficiently. Maintaining a steady cadence within a recommended range can improve your endurance and help prevent fatigue.
- It assists in finding your optimal cadence, the speed at which you pedal most effectively. This cadence varies from person to person.
- It enables you to connect wirelessly to bike computers or smartphones and monitor your pedaling speed in real-time.

A power meter measures the power you generate when cycling, expressed in watts. It tells you precisely how much force you're applying to the pedals, which is directly related to how hard you're working. Power meters can be integrated into various bike parts, such as the crankset, rear wheel hub, or pedals. Here's why they're valuable:

- Unlike other metrics, power is an objective measure of effort unaffected by wind, hills, or other external factors.
- Knowing how much power you produce can tailor your training to improve performance, endurance, and strength.

- It provides immediate feedback about your riding and efforts, enabling you to track your progress and adjust your training accordingly.

Both cadence sensors and power meters provide detailed insights into riding. While a cadence sensor focuses on how fast you're pedaling, a power meter tells you how much effort you put into each pedal stroke.

Do You Need a Cadence Sensor and Power Meter?

Most smart trainers have built-in power meters, and some also have cadence sensors. However, if your trainer doesn't have these features, consider getting separate sensors. They provide valuable data, such as training zones, that help monitor your progress and tailor your training.

I purchased the Zwift Hub; however, at the time of publication, Zwift no longer makes these units. Instead, it sells Wahoo KICKR Core: Zwift One, which includes a one-year Zwift membership and turns your bike into an indoor fitness setup. Indoor trainer apps like Zwift, TrainerRoad and Rouvy offer an excellent way to maintain your cycling regimen during winter or whenever outdoor riding isn't possible. You can embark on an immersive cycling journey from home with the right trainer and a stable internet connection.

QUICK TIPS

- If you are serious about riding, I recommend getting a smart trainer. It will make life much easier by allowing you to use your bike instead of having to go to the gym. It will also emulate a "real" with similarly generated watts. You will become a more efficient rider.
- I enjoy using Zwift, but it can get pricey. Find the program that works best for you.

Matt Fitzgerald
Endurance Coach and Author of *On Pace*, Flagstaff, AZ

At 27, I was an editor for *Triathlete* magazine. Despite my job, I swore off ever participating in a triathlon—that is, until I got invited to a race in sunny St. Maarten.

The tourism board had graciously flown us editors in to cover this triathlon, and in a moment of sheer gratitude (or madness), I decided to join in on the action—an Olympic Triathlon, no less! At that point, I only ran casually, barely biking or swimming.

The day before the race, I rented a mountain bike from a local bike shop that felt as heavy as a boulder. Unbeknownst to me, the derailleur was broken. My preparation also involved a last-minute dip in the hotel pool and a wild night out partying with the other journalists and my girlfriend, now my wife, Nataki.

Race day dawned, and breakfast was a Snickers bar from a gas station. The swim was a complete disaster. By the time I emerged, all the bikes were gone. The jingling car keys in my pocket during the 26-mile ride were a metaphor for my chaotic preparation. Then, I took a nasty fall right in front of the American journalists, earning myself a body full of road rash.

The run that followed was a grueling exercise in humility. It was so hot and soupy that I felt like I was marching towards my death rather than racing. The final indignity came when I was locked in a battle with the septuagenarian race director to avoid coming in last.

As I sprinted past him in the home stretch, Nataki was waiting for me at the finish line, her mouth agape at my bloodied, sweaty state. Greg Gutfeld of *Men's Health* magazine at the time, now at Fox, who was also present, couldn't help but laugh at the sight of the "bloody/sweaty" *Triathlon* magazine editor struggling to avoid last place.

Despite the Red Cross staff's attempts to help, I waved them off and rushed to the airport with Nataki. Since no one was at the rental counter and we needed to catch our flight, we left our car behind. I hobbled down the aisle with our luggage, looking like a scene from a horror movie.

On the flight back to San Diego, battered and bloodied, I made a vow that I was going to participate in the next triathlon I could find. I had to redeem myself. That's how I got hooked.

PART 4

RUNNING

It's important to start at a pace you can sustain. Don't start out too fast at a race. –Gwen Jorgensen

CHAPTER 28

What You Need for Running

"The run portion of a triathlon was a gentle 1.5-mile incline, out and back, so the return was downhill. Like a dummy, I forgot to put on my belt with my race bib. I likely would've been DQ'd for that, except in the last mile of the run, with literally a mile left to go, my right quad locked up and left me lying on the ground in pain, unable to move. I had to be driven to the finish line for my humbling DNF. The one goal I had was to finish. I was already in the last 2-3 finishers. I was so close–utterly pathetic." –Pathetic Triathlete Group Member

Many triathletes get their start as runners. Running is one of the most accessible sports. You don't need much, just a good pair of sneakers to run out the door. But here are some other things you may consider using.

Eyewear

Everyone needs good protective eyewear. Some people wear their prescription glasses. I don't suggest that. If you wear prescription lenses, pick up a pair of sports eyewear. They are made to stay on your face and not bounce around as you run or ride. If you don't wear prescription lenses, a good pair of sunglasses with UV protection is the way to go. I've been loving the ROKA brand sunglasses. They come in prescription and progressive lenses. This lets me see in the distance and look at my watch without switching glasses.

Hydration Belts

Some people like holding a water bottle or hydration in a handheld pouch. I prefer a hydration belt with ample water for my run that can also keep my phone, keys, and a little money. There are so many good hydration belts on the market. I have many favorite belts, including CamelBak, SPI, Arc'teryx, Ultimate Direction, Fitletic, and G-Run.

Socks

The right sock is going to make a huge difference. Plan on spending between $15 and $20 for socks that wick away the sweat and help prevent blisters. Some may like to run in compression socks up to their knees. Compression is great for keeping the circulation going, especially if you have Achilles tendinitis or shin splints. I typically wear compression socks after I run or after I cycle. I find they help speed up recovery. I prefer short socks like CEP, Jogology, Injinji, Balega, and many others during a run.

Sneakers

Finding the right running shoes is crucial, whether you're a seasoned marathoner or a beginner. Wearing the proper sneakers can enhance your performance and prevent injuries.

Understand your foot type. Your foot type significantly influences the running shoe that suits you best. There are three primary foot types: flat, neutral, and high-arched. Each foot type correlates with how much your foot pronates or rolls inward when you run.

Pronation is the foot's natural inward roll following a heel strike. It helps to absorb impact and adapt to different surfaces. There are three types of pronation:

- If your foot rolls too far inward, you are an overpronator. This is common in people with flat feet and may lead to injuries such as shin splints or plantar fasciitis. Stability or motion-control shoes can help correct overpronation.
- If your foot doesn't roll inward enough, you underpronate. This is often seen in individuals with high arches and can result in stress-related injuries due to reduced impact absorption. Cushioned or neutral shoes can help.
- If your foot rolls inward at an optimal degree, you have neutral pronation. Most running shoes are designed for neutral runners.

Neutral vs. Stability Shoes

Neutral Shoes are designed for runners with neutral pronation or slight underpronation. They offer some shock absorption and medial (arch-side) support. Neutral shoes include Nike Air Pegasus, Adidas UltraBoost, Brooks Ghost, HOKA Clifton, Skechers GO RUN Ride, and New Balance Fresh Foam.

Stability Shoes—These are intended for runners with mild-to-moderate overpronation. They often include a firm "post" in the midsole to reinforce the arch side, an area highly impacted by overpronation. Examples include Skechers GO RUN Forza, Brooks Adrenaline, and New Balance 860 v12.

Bob Cook, triathlete and owner of Runner's Edge Running Store on Long Island, New York, said, "My best advice for new runners is to make sure your new sneakers are not too small. I see way too many beginners buying the wrong size. That is why it is important to have a running store analyze your foot and put you in the right shoe."

Get a Professional Fitting

Visit a specialty running store, like Runner's Roost in Colorado, to get professionally fitted for your running shoes. The store can analyze your gait and foot type and recommend suitable shoes. However, not all running stores offer this service. Before you go, call around to ensure they do.

Try Before You Buy

Always try on shoes before purchasing them. If possible, test them in the store on a treadmill. The best time to try running shoes is in the afternoon or after a workout, as feet swell during the day. Some running stores, like Road Runner Sports, allow you to try out the shoes for 30 days, and if you don't like them, you can return them for store credit.

Replacing Your Running Shoes

Running shoes should be replaced every 300-500 miles, as the cushioning wears out over time. Tracking your mileage can help you know when it's time for a new pair. If you don't, you can get shin splints or something worse. I've seen people wear out their shoes, and it's not good for their feet or legs. Make sure you don't get to that point.

Should You Have More Than One Pair of Sneakers?

I like having a pair of sneakers that I race in and a pair to train in. Here are my suggestions: Skechers, Brooks, HOKA, New Balance, and so many other brands that I love. The Skora and Xero zero-drop shoes are very comfortable. However, they are considered barefoot shoes, so I use them for specific training, like track runs.

Training sneakers, also known as everyday running shoes, are designed to be durable and provide maximum support and cushioning. They are built to withstand high mileage runs and daily use, making them more substantial and heavier.

Training sneakers absorb the impact of running on hard surfaces and reduce the risk of injury. They also typically offer more support to help keep feet comfortable during long runs. Training shoes are generally versatile and can handle various workouts, from long runs to speed drills. For example, I train in my HOKA Skyflow, Brooks Ghost, and Skechers Aero Burst. But I'm constantly changing it up with different brands.

On the other hand, racing sneakers are designed for competitive runners looking to achieve their personal best times. They are lighter and more minimalistic than training shoes. The most noticeable characteristic of racing shoes is their weight. They're made from lightweight materials to minimize your load, allowing you to run faster. Racing shoes usually have less cushioning than training shoes. This design aspect makes them lighter but also means they provide less shock absorption. With their lightweight design and minimal cushioning, racing shoes are built for speed and efficiency. They're intended for use in races or speed workouts, where the goal is to run fast. For racing, I like to wear my adidas Adizero Adios Pro 3, Nike Zoom Fly, and the TYR Valkyrie Elite Carbon Runner.

Do You Need Insoles?

Insoles can be a game changer for runners, providing the extra support and cushioning that standard running shoes might lack. They are particularly beneficial for those with specific foot issues, such as flat feet, high arches, or plantar fasciitis, offering customized comfort to help prevent injuries and enhance overall performance. Insoles can also improve the alignment of your legs and hips, reducing stress on joints and muscles.

However, not every runner needs them. You might not require additional inserts if your shoes provide adequate support and you don't experience discomfort or injuries. It's important to assess your needs and consult a specialist to determine if insoles could significantly improve your running experience.

Because of my high arches, I like running with insoles. There are so many fantastic companies out there that make excellent insoles. Make sure to check them out at your favorite local running store.

QUICK TIPS

- Finding the right running shoes is an individualized process. Typically, you'll want to focus on your foot type, pronation, and personal comfort before you purchase new sneakers.
- You should have a training shoe and a racing shoe. Remember to replace them every 300+ miles. If you don't, you could experience shin splints or other types of injuries.

How to Dress for the Weather?

0°F–20°F: Very Cold

If you must run in this weather, wear layers. If you have respiratory disease or asthma, skip the outdoor workout and hit the gym instead.

- Base Layer: Start with a moisture-wicking base layer to keep sweat away from your skin. Then, wear a long-sleeved top and thermal tights.
- Mid-Layer: Add an insulating mid-layer, like a fleece pullover, to retain heat.
- Outer Layer: A wind- and water-resistant jacket will protect you from wind chill and snow.
- Accessories: Wear thermal socks, gloves or mittens, a hat or headband, and a neck gaiter or scarf. If it's especially frigid, consider wearing a face mask or balaclava. I love the Turtle Gloves. They work great for running, and they have ones for frigid to 50 degrees Fahrenheit weather!

20°F–40°F: Cold

Less layering is needed as the temperature increases, but still dress warmly.

- Base Layer: Stick with the moisture-wicking long-sleeved top and tights.
- Outer Layer: Wear a jacket or windbreaker, depending on the wind chill.
- Accessories: Wear thermal socks, gloves, and a hat or headband.

40°F–60°F: Cool to Mild

This range is generally comfortable for running.

- Upper Body: A long-sleeved technical shirt should be enough. If it's closer to 40 degrees Fahrenheit, consider a light jacket.

- Lower Body: Running tights or shorts, depending on your preference and the exact temperature.
- Accessories: Gloves might be needed if it's closer to 40 degrees Fahrenheit.

60°F–80°F: Warm

As the temperature rises, less clothing is necessary.

- Upper Body: A short-sleeved, moisture-wicking shirt will keep you cool.
- Lower Body: Shorts are the best option.
- Accessories: A hat or visor can protect your face from the sun.

80°F–100°F: Hot to Very Hot

In these temperatures, protecting yourself from overheating and the sun is crucial.

- Upper Body: Opt for a tank top or a lightweight, moisture-wicking, breathable shirt.
- Lower Body: Go for shorts to maximize heat escape.
- Accessories: Wear a hat or visor, sunglasses, and sunscreen. If it's extremely hot, consider a cooling towel.

CHAPTER 29

How to Run-Walk

"I once packed my wife's sneakers for a Kingston, New York triathlon. It was too late to return to the house, so I tried a Hail Mary, approached the race director, and asked if he could announce over the PA system if anyone had an extra pair of size 12 sneakers. I also explained why I was in that predicament, which, it turns out, was a mistake. The race director obliged and promptly got on the PA, stating, 'Can anyone help this poor guy? He brought his wife's sneakers by mistake.' After getting over my embarrassment, I found that there was someone with sneakers in my size. That saved me from running in my Crocs." –WeREndurance Member

When I started running in 2011, I didn't realize I was doing run-walk. I would race to the water stop, take a break, and then run to the next water stop and take a break.

When I was accepted into the NYC Marathon in 2016, Jeff Galloway was my first call. Jeff, a former Olympian who coined the term "run-walk-run," was someone I met a few times at the RunDisney events and was enamored with. He had written several books and was already blogging for me.

I asked Jeff how to get started to train for a marathon. Jeff offered to coach me. He helped me through my plantar fasciitis, Achilles tendinitis, knee pain, and more. He was gentle and taught me the run-walk method, a simple but effective approach to running that incorporates walking intervals into runs.

The principle behind this method is to give runners control over their workouts, making it an ideal way to increase fitness with planned recovery breaks. The idea is that the planned walk breaks are a form of active recovery that allows you to catch your breath, reduce fatigue, and prepare for the next running interval.

When you run, you RUN. When you walk, you walk at a normal pace. You don't speedwalk.

To start using the run-walk method, find your baseline. This involves warming up at a slow pace with some drills. The drills include an accelerator glider where you run for 15 seconds, run faster for 15 seconds, and then go all out for 15 seconds before recovery with a 30-second walk. The other drills include a shuffle drill where you run on your toes for 15 seconds and then recover with a 30-second walk. The final drill includes a cadence drill, where you count your left foot every time it strikes down. Then, a 30-second walk. Do this several times and try to beat each time by counting 2–6 more foot strokes.

For a time trial and to learn your pacing, go to a track and warm up. After that, take the first quarter mile (one time around the track) easy, then speed it up on the second go-around. The third time around, go faster; for the last quarter mile, go all out! On jeffgalloway.com, you can add your time, and it will calculate your pace and estimated results for a 5K, 10K, half marathon, or full marathon.

The run-walk method is beneficial for everyone. I recommend starting with a run-walk if you are a beginner, an advanced runner, or someone with chronic injuries. You will thank me for it. Using the run-walk method, you will get fewer injuries and recover faster. I have runners in my group who run at a 7- or 8-minute/mile pace using the run-walk method, so it's accessible to all runners.

Drills

Here are some additional drills. Do these for ten minutes altogether. Ten minutes is a good warm-up before a run.

High Knees

High Knees help improve your stride rate and knee lift. While standing tall, march in place, lifting your knees as high as possible. Try to do this drill for about 30–60 seconds.

Butt Kick Drill

The Butt Kick Drill activates and stretches the quadriceps, increases heart rate, and enhances overall leg flexibility, preparing the body for the activity ahead. Jog forward while kicking your heel up toward your glutes. Your knee should stay pointed down as you do this drill.

A-Skips

A-Skips are great for improving coordination and foot strike. In this drill, you skip like when you were a child.

Strides

Strides help you practice running fast and relaxed. Start by jogging, then gradually accelerate to about 95% of your full speed and gradually decelerate. Each stride should take about 20–30 seconds.

Carioca

Carioca, also known as the grapevine, helps improve hip flexibility and balance. To move laterally, continuously step your trailing leg in front and behind you.

Heel-To-Toe Walk

Heel-to-Toe Walk drill helps stretch and warm your calves. Walk forward slowly, placing your weight on your heel and rolling forward onto your toes.

Run-Walk Pacing

Many people who run/walk enjoy the 30-second run/30-second walk interval. Those intervals need to be faster for me. I prefer a shorter walk, like 15 seconds. For example, if I run for 30 seconds, I walk for 15 seconds. For the longer running intervals, like a minute or more, I will walk for 30 seconds. Try different intervals and see what works for you. But don't take a longer break than 30 seconds. Also, pick up a Gymboss timer from Amazon or buy one on Jeff Galloway's website. Jeff also offers a Run Walk Run® app which includes a run-walk timer. The app is available for both iOS and Adroid.

QUICK TIPS

- Consider running-walking during your run portion of the triathlon, especially if you are doing an Olympic-, half-, or full-distance triathlon.
- You can try different run-walk intervals.

CHAPTER 30

Types of Running Workouts

"I took my timing chip off to take off my wetsuit. I started on the bike without it. It wasn't until I got out on the run that I realized I didn't have it on. I had to run back to Transition to grab it. I wasn't sure the whole run whether my finish would count. Luckily, it did, and I won my age group!"
–Pathetic Triathlete Member

If you decide to run-walk or just straight run, there are many different workouts that you can incorporate into your training program. Here are some:

Interval Runs

Interval Runs involve running hard for a set amount of time or distance, followed by a period of easy recovery jogging or walking. For example, one might run for one minute at a hard effort, recover with two minutes of easy jogging, and repeat the workout 10 times.

Tempo Runs

Tempo Runs are sustained efforts at a challenging but manageable pace. You should be able to talk in short phrases, but only hold part of the conversation. A sample workout might include a 10-minute easy warm-up, 20 minutes at a tempo pace, and a 10-minute cool-down.

Fartlek Runs

Fartlek Runs, also known in Swedish as "speed play," involves changing your pace throughout your run. After a warm-up, you might run hard (Zone 4) to the next mailbox, easy (Zone 1) to the next stop sign, and so on. Please do this for the entire workout, whether 30 minutes or one hour, and have fun with it.

Hill Repeats

Hill Repeat is a workout that uses a hill. Find a hill with a moderate incline. Run up for 30 seconds at an arduous effort, then jog or walk back down for recovery. Repeat 10 times.

Long Slow Distance

Long, slow-distance runs are done at a leisurely, conversational pace and help build endurance. They should be done at a Zone 1 pace. The distance will depend on your current fitness level and goals.

Progression Run

The progression run begins at a comfortable pace, and then your speed gradually increases, making the last mile a hard effort.

Track Workouts

Track Workouts are great for precise interval workouts. For example, run 400 meters (one lap on most tracks) after a warm-up at a hard effort, followed by 400 meters of easy recovery jogging. Repeat four times.

Recovery Runs

Recovery Runs are shorter, easier runs after a hard workout or race. They should be done at an effortless, relaxed pace.

Structuring Your Run Workouts

Try to do a different workout every day. Too many people do an easy or a hard run daily and continue the same route. The problem is that you will not see improvements if you keep the same pace and distance. But if you add intervals and some of these other workouts, you will see improvements quickly.

Break It Up

I like to run every other day. Each workout should be different. One day, I may do a Fartlek workout, and the next time I run, I will do strides or an easy run.

Many of your runs should be easy. However, if you want to get faster, you must also incorporate speed workouts.

Sample 2-Week Workout

Remember to refer to chapter 10 on Understanding Training Zones before trying this out.

	Tuesday	Thursday	Saturday
Week 1	Track workout, Tempo run with cadence drills (30-40 minutes)	Hill Repeats (30 minutes)	Long Run in Zone 1 (1 hour)
Week 2	Fartlek Run (30 minutes)	Recovery Run Z1/Z2 (30-40 minutes)	Long Run Zone 1 (90 minutes)

QUICK TIPS

- Break up your workouts. Don't do the same one every time you run.
- Incorporate speed workouts to help you run faster.

Running Etiquette

Basic Etiquette

- Stay alert to your environment, including other runners, cyclists, pedestrians, and vehicles.
- Obey all traffic signals and signs. Run on designated paths or sidewalks where available.
- If you run on the road, run against traffic so you will see who is coming. If they are not slowing down, move over quickly.
- Stay to the right side of the path (or the left, if running in the UK), allowing faster runners or cyclists to pass on the left.
- When passing another runner, do so on the left and announce your presence with a simple "On your left" or "Passing on your left." (if you live in the UK, announce that you are passing on the right.)
- If running in a group, avoid running more than two abreast to keep pathways clear for others.
- If you wear headphones or earbuds, ensure you can hear the outside world.

Trail Running

- Follow all posted signs and regulations specific to the trail you are on.
- If you're on multi-use trails, yield to uphill runners, hikers, and equestrians.
- Stick to marked trails to prevent environmental damage and avoid getting lost.
- Carry all trash and leave the environment as you found it. Don't disturb wildlife or plants.

Race Etiquette

- At the starting line, position yourself according to your expected pace. Faster runners should be at the front, while slower runners and walkers should be toward the back.
- If you need to stop or walk, move to the side and raise your hand high to avoid causing collisions.
- At aid stations, grab your drink and keep moving. If you need to stop, move out of the way first.
- Acknowledge and thank race volunteers and officials. They play a crucial role in the event's success.

Courtesy and Safety

- If you listen to music while running, keep the volume low or use one earbud to stay aware of your surroundings.
- Use hand signals or verbal cues to indicate turns, stops, or hazards.
- A simple wave, nod, or smile to other runners and pedestrians can foster a positive running community.
- If you're carrying water or snacks, make sure not to litter. Dispose of waste properly.

CHAPTER 31

Running Technique and Form

"During my first triathlon, I marked myself. While on the run, I was getting some strange looks from others. As I passed another runner, she asked me, "Are you really 69? You look great for your age!" I couldn't figure out why she thought I was 69 (I was 47). Later, I realized I had marked my leg with my race number and not my age." –Pathetic Triathlete Member

Running involves good coordination, strength, and the ability to keep going for a long time. Although everyone runs differently, some general tips can make running easier and help avoid injury.

The Importance of Good Running Form

Good running form is about more than just looking graceful on the move. It's a critical factor in improving performance and preventing injuries. When you run with proper form, you maximize your body's efficiency, allowing you to run faster, farther, and with less fatigue.

Posture

Good running form begins with posture. It starts at the head and travels through the body. Keep your head up, looking forward, and your neck and shoulders relaxed. Avoid slumping or hunching over, which can restrict breathing and lead to shoulder tension. Lastly, tilt your body slightly forward and lean ever so slightly.

Arm Swing

Your arms should swing naturally with each step, moving forward and backward, not across your body. The angle in your elbow should be about 90 degrees. Keep your hands relaxed. Don't tighten up.

Foot Strike

There's an ongoing debate among runners and coaches about whether it's better to land on the heel, midfoot, or forefoot. However, most experts agree that the most important thing is for your foot to land under your body rather than out in front of it to avoid overstriding.

In addition, trying to land on your midfoot or forefoot takes a lot of pressure off your knees, which can be a problem if you have issues with them.

Cadence

Cadence, as it refers to running, is the number of steps you take per minute. Increasing your cadence can improve your efficiency and reduce impact forces. A typical target for an elite athlete is 180 steps per minute, but this varies and is hard to achieve. By counting your left foot for 15 seconds, you can multiply that by four and know your cadence. If you are well below 130, you must shorten your stride. You do this by striking your feet closer together.

Breathing

Coordinate your breathing with your steps to maintain a steady, rhythmic pattern. Many runners find a pattern of two steps (one left, one right) for each inhale and two for each exhale. Some runners find nose breathing beneficial. It regulates their breathing, enhances filtration, lowers their heart rate, and promotes calmness. However, it is not easy to do this. My advice is to do what works for you.

Putting It All Together

Improving your running technique takes time and conscious effort. Start by focusing on one aspect at a time, such as your posture or arm swing. Once you've improved one area, move on to the next.

Everyone's optimal running form will look slightly different due to factors like body type and running style. The goal is not to achieve a "perfect" form but an efficient and effective one for you.

QUICK TIPS

- You should start to notice your form. You may want to have someone film you so that you can see exactly what you are doing and look for ways to improve.
- Make sure you figure out your cadence to know how to improve.

Jon Lipshie
Triathlete, Wilmington, DE

At 61, I competed in my first triathlon, the Smith Point Triathlon, organized by EventPower LI.

My journey began in November 2020 during the COVID-19 pandemic, when I decided to start swimming at my local YMCA. I gradually built up my endurance to cover 500 meters, which proved to be a challenging feat.

I owned a hybrid bike without clips and had some running experience. However, the swimming segment filled me with anxiety leading up to the event.

Although I had practiced open water swimming at Tobay Beach and the Great South Bay, dealing with currents, unpredictable weather, a mass start, and a rocky sea floor was daunting.

My worries were heightened by the fact that I wore glasses, and my goggles were not prescription, leaving me virtually blind in the water.

Despite my apprehension, I felt a surge of confidence on the day of the event. However, within 100 yards of the swim, I lost my goggles. I don't know how that happened.

By the time I emerged from the water, I was emotionally drained. Removing my full wetsuit took me six minutes, and the long run from the water through the parking lot to transition was exhausting.

Once I mounted my bike, though, the fun began! I felt strong on the flat course. The only hiccup was that I initially rode too swiftly, leaving me struggling with depleted energy against the wind on the return journey.

Transitioning from the bike to the run was seamless. It was startling to see many participants walking, looking as weary as characters from "The Walking Dead."

In contrast, I felt energized. I seized the opportunity to overtake others during the run, and by the time I completed the 5K run, I felt fantastic.

Training for the triathlon was demanding, akin to preparing for my first marathon. During the event, you temporarily forget your struggles, but crossing the finish line brings a rush of exhilaration that makes every effort worthwhile.

CHAPTER 32

How to Run Faster

"I raced a sprint and decided not to wear socks. I had trained my run without them, and it was no problem. But I forgot to train on the bike. The combination of wet ankles and cycling shoes rubbed big blisters into my ankles. After a mile of torture, my shoes came off when I got out for the run, and I ran the rest of the 5k barefoot on hot South Louisiana pavement." –Pathetic Triathlete Member

Running faster involves more than just trying harder. It combines both body and mind work. You must use the right techniques to get quicker, follow a training plan, and think positively about overcoming challenges.

Speed training is key to improving your record or winning against others. Starting this process means strengthening your body, improving your running, and using methods that help you move faster and endure more.

The first step in increasing your speed is to increase your stride turnover, which is the number of steps you take per minute. To practice, run for 30 seconds faster than your current pace, then jog or walk for a minute to recover, and repeat.

Interval training involves alternating between periods of high-intensity running and recovery. One method is to add sprints to your long runs. Start with a warm-up, sprint for a set distance or time, then reduce your speed to a comfortable jog or walk to recover. Repeat this cycle throughout your run.

Hills can be your secret weapon for increasing speed. Find a hill or use a treadmill with an incline setting and run up and down the hill repeatedly. This helps build strength and endurance, directly translating into flat terrain speed.

Finally, stay consistent with your training routine to improve your speed. However, you must also take rest days so your body can recover and rebuild stronger, allowing you to run faster over time.

Running with a group can motivate you to push your pace, helping you run faster.

In my run-walk group, we work on building endurance. We run-walk at a gentle pace and build mileage weekly. I have found that the slower I go on long runs, the faster I run at a race.

QUICK TIPS

- Improving your running speed requires consistent training, proper technique, and adequate recovery.
- Incorporating these can help you gradually increase your pace and enjoy the thrill of running faster.

CHAPTER 33

Common Running Injuries

"It wasn't me, but a participant in our triathlon. He was in the lead, turned at the wrong buoy, and swam in. Got to shore and had to go back out and swim to and around the correct buoy. Another option was DQ. He still came in like 5th or 6th!!" –Pathetic Triathlete Member

Getting injured is part of the triathlon experience. Although you can get injured swimming and cycling, running injuries are much more common. Regular stretching improves flexibility and range of motion and prevents injuries.

Craig DiGiovanni, Founding Partner of Medi-Dyne, said, "Proper stretching can prevent most common running injuries and often resolve them."

Here are some common running injuries and what you can do about them.

Runner's Knee (Patellofemoral Pain Syndrome)

A runner's knee is characterized by pain around or behind the kneecap. Overuse, muscle imbalances, or kneecap misalignment often cause it. Strengthening exercises for the hips, hamstrings, and quads can help prevent this condition. See a specialist to find out what options are best for you.

In my experience, wearing a compression sleeve, such as the GO Sleeves Knee Compression with built-in K-tape, is helpful when addressing knee issues.

Stress Fractures

Stress fractures are small cracks in the bone that occur over time due to repetitive force, often from overuse, such as repeatedly jumping up and down or running long distances. Rest and cross-training activities that don't put weight on the affected bone are crucial for recovery.

Shin Splints

Shin splints cause pain along the shinbone (tibia). They're often linked to sudden changes in physical activity, such as increasing mileage too quickly. Rest, ice, and over-the-counter pain relievers can help alleviate symptoms. Proper footwear and strength training can also help prevent shin splints.

I have found that people who wear the same sneakers for years develop shin splints. Make sure to replace your sneakers every few hundred miles and wear compression sleeves to aid recovery.

Achilles Tendinopathy

This injury involves the Achilles tendon, which connects the two primary calf muscles to the back of the heel. Overuse can lead to inflammation and pain. Treatment usually involves rest, ice, and exercises to strengthen the calf muscles.

Plantar Fasciitis

Plantar fasciitis is inflammation of the plantar fascia, the thick band of tissue that connects your heel bone to your toes. It's common in runners and can cause a stabbing pain in the heel. Rest, ice, and stretching can help manage symptoms. Use a firm ball and roll it on your heel. If pain persists, see a podiatrist.

Iliotibial Band Syndrome

The iliotibial band is a piece of connective tissue that runs from the hip to the knee. Overuse can cause it to become inflamed, leading to pain on the outside of the knee. Treatment often involves rest, ice, and stretching. Strengthening the hips and glutes can also help alleviate and prevent this issue.

"It's important to seek medical advice to make sure there isn't anything more serious going on," says Sharon Levy, MSPT, Co-Owner of Excel PT and Workout in Manhasset, NY. "Going to a physical therapist is very helpful. We try to determine the underlying cause of your issue. During the evaluation, we look for abnormal movement patterns, faulty posture, imbalances, and deficiencies in both strength and flexibility. A personalized program is then developed to correct any problems and optimize your performance in sports. We want you to get back out there and do your thing better than ever."

If you're experiencing persistent pain or discomfort, seek professional medical advice. Proper warm-ups, cool-downs, strength training exercises, listening to your body, and resting when needed are key to staying injury-free.

QUICK TIPS

- At some point, you will get injured. It's okay. Dust yourself off and get back out there.
- Listen to your body. Don't push through abnormal pain! You can damage yourself even more.
- If you are injured, go to an orthopedist, physical therapist, chiropractor, or podiatrist (depending on the injury).

Chris Gannon
Triathlete, Owner of Bolay Fresh Bold Kitchen, Jupiter, FL

Although I've always been athletic, I never considered myself an endurance athlete. Running and biking were passions of mine, but swimming was not a regular activity in my routine.

My interest in triathlons sparked when my wife and sister decided to participate in their first sprint triathlon. Watching them compete and the camaraderie among the athletes inspired me to give it a try.

So, at 33, I registered for the Trilogy Triathlon in Miami. This sprint triathlon was a 600-yard swim, a 13-mile bike ride, and a 5K run. Lacking formal training, I relied on YouTube videos to learn about transitioning between different race stages.

Race day presented unique challenges. The bay's salty water made the swim tough, but the rest of the course was manageable, mostly flat with a few bridges. Despite the hurdles, I thoroughly enjoyed the experience.

Following my first triathlon, I encouraged my team from Bolay Fresh Bold Kitchen, where I work, to participate. Triathlons hold a special charm. You don't need to be an Ironman to call yourself a triathlete. Anyone who competes in a multisport event earns that title.

Reflecting on my journey and seeing how my strengths have shifted is interesting. Initially, biking was my strong suit, but now, I excel in swimming.

Success in triathlons hinges on accountability. Having a supportive community or a coach can make a significant difference.

What I love most about triathlons is how they shape character and resilience. There's a peculiar satisfaction in enduring the pain because it refines you as a person. For instance, competing in Alcatraz was a formidable challenge. I've done it four times, braving four-foot swells in 50-degree Fahrenheit Bay waters, negotiating hilly terrains in the rain, and running through an obstacle course that included sand. It's brutally tough but instills a character strength permeating all aspects of life.

CHAPTER 34

The Power of Walking

"During my second triathlon, I still hadn't figured out nutrition. I bonked on the bike and stood on the side of the road (about a mile from the transition area), gulping my sports drink that did not have many calories in it. Walked about a 1/4 mile and finally got on the bike and limped in. No part of me wanted to 'run', especially when a good chunk of the course was in soft sand. But the song blasting over the speakers had the lyrics 'you're not done yet.' So, I walked 5 miles, finished DFL, and promptly fell apart, bawling. Still can't find that song. I kinda think I hallucinated it." –Pathetic Triathlete Member

Triathlons are grueling tests of endurance that require the ability to swim, bike, and run long distances without rest. To compete effectively, triathletes must be in peak physical condition. However, even the most dedicated athletes can experience injuries or recovery periods where running is not an option. Walking can become a potent tool in your training arsenal in such situations.

Walking, often underestimated, is remarkably like running in terms of its biomechanics. Both activities engage the same muscle groups, require forward motion, and use the cardiovascular system.

The primary difference lies in the intensity and impact on the joints. Walking offers a lower-impact alternative, making it an excellent activity for those recovering from injuries or seeking a gentler exercise during recovery periods.

The advantages of walking extend beyond its low-impact nature. A brisk walk can improve cardiovascular fitness, strengthen bones, reduce excess body fat, and boost muscle power and endurance. (After I had my daughter, I walked every day and quickly lost the extra weight that I gained when I was pregnant.)

Research suggests that walking improves mental well-being, reduces stress, anxiety, and fatigue. It can also serve as a stepping stone for running. If you can comfortably walk a certain distance, you can run it, too. For instance, if you can walk four miles easily, you're likely capable of running the same distance.

Walking is highly beneficial for those returning from an injury. By starting with walking, you can gradually rebuild your stamina and strength until you're ready to resume running, reducing the risk of re-injury.

Incorporating walking into your training routine can also increase your overall mileage without significantly increasing the risk of overuse injuries.

For triathletes looking to build endurance, adding walking sessions to their training schedule can help them safely increase their weekly mileage.

Walking is more than a "fallback" option when running is off the table. It's a valuable training tool. By harnessing the power of walking, triathletes can maintain their fitness levels during recovery periods, reduce the risk of injury, and build a solid foundation for running.

I like to wear the HOKA Bondi sneaker when walking, but there are many great brands on the market. Find something supportive that will work for you.

QUICK TIPS

- Walking is an excellent way to help you recover from an injury or illness.
- Don't "pooh-pooh" walking. If you can walk 10 miles, you can run 10 miles!

PART 5

TRIATHLON

Before the race, look at the course. Is it hilly? Is it flat? Whatever it is, practice on that terrain. –Gwen Jorgensen

CHAPTER 35

How to Structure Your Training

"During my first sprint distance triathlon, I was getting annoyed at my helmet sitting too low on my head and sliding down the front. Ten kilometers into the 20k ride, I realized I had put my helmet on backward."
–Pathetic Triathlete Member

Triathlon training requires careful planning. You must organize your training schedule in advance, consider how to balance the three disciplines, manage your time effectively, and ensure you're getting the right mix of endurance, strength, and recovery. This helps improve performance and avoid injuries.

It's important to know about periodization to train well for a triathlon. Periodization refers to breaking down your training into distinct periods or cycles. Each cycle focuses on different workouts to gradually improve your fitness and skills without burning out or getting injured. This way, you build up your ability step by step, getting ready for the race in the best possible way.

What Is Your "A" Race?

Determine your "A" race for the season. An "A" race is the main race that a triathlete focuses on and gives the most importance to during their training season. It's the one they want to do their best in, so they plan their training to be in top shape for this race. You may have two "A" races, but probably one is enough.

Once you determine your "A" races, figure out what other races you will add to your training. These races are considered your "B" or "C" races. The "B" is not as important as the "A," but is still important. You want to do your best during this race. The "C" race is done more for fun and fitness.

Macrocycle

The entire training cycle is referred to as a "macrocycle." This can be a year-long program. This broad overview is crucial as it sets the stage for the overall goals, major competitions, and the progression of training phases.

The macrocycle is divided into two- to three-week training blocks, each focusing on endurance, strength, speed, and recovery. These blocks are designed to progressively build your fitness and performance while allowing adequate recovery to prevent overtraining.

Example: Say you plan to race in Ironman, NY, in September, but it's currently January. From January to May, the focus will be on consistency, and you may want to have one or two block workouts where you focus on a single activity instead of three, allowing you to improve in that area. Then, from May to September, you will have harder training every 3 weeks, followed by one week of recovery training. This will last until just about a month before your event, when you start to taper and reduce your training.

Mesocycle

The mesocycle is shorter than a macrocycle, typically lasting about four weeks. A common approach is to structure this in a 3:1 ratio, with three weeks of built-in fitness and one week of recovery. (When I say recovery, I don't mean taking off altogether. It's a little easier with a lighter week during the block.) This pattern has been proven effective in developing fitness while ensuring sufficient rest and recovery.

During the first three weeks of the cycle, the volume and intensity of training gradually increase. This is known as progressive overload, a fundamental principle for enhancing endurance, speed, and strength. The fourth week, also known as the recovery week, is when the volume and intensity are significantly reduced. This allows your body to recover, adapt, and return stronger for the next mesocycle.

Microcycle

The microcycle is the smallest unit of the training plan, typically spanning seven days. It is your weekly training schedule, the most detailed level of your training plan, where you decide on the specific workouts for each day of the week.

A typical microcycle includes workout types such as long endurance sessions, HIIT, strength and conditioning exercises, technique drills, and rest days. It's important to balance these different types of workouts to ensure a well-rounded training program.

For example, you may want to structure your training as follows:

Monday	Tuesday	Wednesday	Thursday	Friday	Saturday	Sunday
Day off	Hard bike/ followed by run off the bike	Swimming longer/ harder with intervals, followed by Strength	Easy bike (60 minutes)	Swimming (1 hour) followed by Strength	Long ride (90 minutes)	Long run (90 minutes)

Block Training

Block training in triathlon is a specific type of training periodization where you focus intensively on one discipline, such as swimming, biking, or running, for a certain period, usually a week or more, while maintaining the other two disciplines.

Block training creates a temporary imbalance in your training, focusing on one sport to see significant improvement in that area. For example, focusing on cycling might double your usual cycling mileage for a week while keeping your swimming and running workouts at a maintenance level.

This approach can effectively address weaknesses or build strength in a particular discipline. After concentrating on one sport for a block, you would then switch and focus on another sport in the next block.

However, it's essential to remember that block training can be quite intense and physically demanding. It requires careful planning and monitoring to prevent overtraining or injury. Always ensure you're allowing your body adequate recovery time between high-intensity or high-volume sessions.

Block training might be used during specific phases of the macrocycle or mesocycle when you want to make substantial gains in one discipline. As with all aspects of triathlon training, block training should be tailored to your individual goals, fitness level, and training schedule.

Structuring triathlon training involves planning. From the broad overview of the macrocycle to the detailed daily plan of the microcycle, each level plays a crucial role in your overall performance. This is why it may make sense to hire a coach. A coach will pull all this together for you.

Understanding how to structure your training using macrocycles, mesocycles, and microcycles can help you optimize your training, prevent burnout, and reach your triathlon goals.

QUICK TIPS

- Your whole training is considered a macrocycle. Be sure to schedule your dates in a calendar and plan your events accordingly.
- Determine your "A" race and build a schedule around that in blocks.
- If you need to focus on one area, consider doing block training.

Stacey Kiefer
Triathlete, Competitive Swimmer, Coach, and Managing Director of Zealios, Bend, OR

My journey into triathlons began in my junior year of college. As a competitive swimmer from Racine, Wisconsin, and a NCAA Division III athlete, I decided to maintain my fitness during the off-season by participating in a triathlon.

Confident in my swimming abilities, I signed up for the 1999 Danskin Triathlon in Naperville, Illinois, at Centennial Beach Park. This event was later rebranded as the Iron Girl Tri Series. I anticipated that an all-women sprint triathlon would be straightforward.

The swimming segment took place in a quarry rather than an open-water swim, presenting a unique challenge with several winding laps.

I purchased a 12-speed Schwinn bicycle and equipped it with aluminum aero bars for the cycling part. My pedals were caged, which, in retrospect, was quite risky. I assumed these modifications would give me an edge in transition speed.

As expected, I excelled in the swim, skillfully maneuvering through the crowd. This experience taught me the importance of positioning myself at the front, a lesson I carried forward to future triathlons.

When I emerged from the swim, I was already wearing shorts I had bought from Kohl's over my swimsuit. They were super wet. Then, on the ride-and-run, it felt like I was running in a diaper, an uncomfortable experience that underscored the importance of choosing the right gear.

Despite these early hiccups, I ascended to an elite triathlon level. This status meant I was often the first out of the water, chased down during the bike ride, my weakest segment, and had to push hard on the run.

I relished the challenge and went on to compete in dozens more triathlons, each one fueling my love for the sport even more.

CHAPTER 36

Triathlon Training

"Imagine Dragon's *Whatever It Takes* played at the last aid station on the Ironman Mt Tremblant 2019 run. I sang it in my head to the finish. It still gets me fired up! Though pathetically, I was singing the wrong lyrics in my head! Lol." –Pathetic Triathlete Member

Now that you know how to swim, bike, and run, it's time to put it all together to gear up for your triathlon training.

Building the Foundation

Before starting specific triathlon training, establish a fitness base in each discipline. Start with short sessions of swimming, cycling, and running, gradually increasing the duration and intensity. The key here is consistency, which will help you develop the stamina needed for a triathlon.

Try to train every day with one day off for rest. Initially, you can do two swims, two bikes, and two weekly runs. As you progress through the season, do three swims, bikes, and runs. There may be days when you will have two workouts in one day. Some require you to complete them simultaneously, like, for example, a brick. A brick is two activities back-to-back, as if you are building a foundation or a house. Most bricks will include a bike and a run. Other workouts can be done in the morning and then after work.

Create a Balanced Training Plan

A balanced training plan should include all three disciplines, ensuring you're prepared for every race phase. A typical week might consist of two days of each discipline and a rest day. Strength training and flexibility exercises should be included in your plan as they can help prevent injuries.

Let's look at a plan. Say you have 20 weeks for your first sprint triathlon and have never done any prior training. You may have a running background, know how to bike, and have been taught to swim as a child. What do you do?

The plan below provides a general outline to give you an idea of what training could entail. The back of the book also contains a few specific training programs for sprint and Olympic races.

Weeks 1–4: Building the Foundation

During the first 4 weeks, focus on building a solid fitness base, keeping the intensity low to moderate.

Weeks 5–8: Increasing Endurance

In this phase, increase the duration of your workouts to build endurance. Add longer, lower-intensity sessions and shorter, higher-intensity sessions.

Weeks 9–12: Building Strength and Speed

Now that you've built a solid base and improved your endurance, it's time to work on speed. For each discipline, incorporate interval training into one of your weekly workouts.

Weeks 13–16: Increasing Intensity

In this phase, focus on race-specific training. This includes practicing transitions and doing brick workouts.

Weeks 17–20: Peak Training and Tapering

In the final four weeks, begin to taper your training by reducing volume while maintaining intensity, allowing your body to recover before the race.

Do a few light workouts and rest in the last week before the race. Pace yourself on race day, hydrate, and, most importantly, enjoy the experience!

Brick Workouts

As stated above, a brick workout refers to doing back-to-back workouts. A brick usually includes a long bike ride followed by a short run. Many people dislike practicing brick workouts because they are challenging and require a lot of effort. After a long bike ride, your legs are shot and feel like Jell-O. Getting used to the brick workout will prepare you for the race, so incorporate these as much as possible. I like to do them whenever I ride, even if it's a short run.

Practice Transitions

Transitions can make or break a triathlon race. The time during transition counts toward your overall performance in the race. Take time to practice moving from swimming to cycling and cycling to running. Efficient transitions can save you valuable time during the race and allow you to take additional time if needed.

Many people get held up in the transitions. They may do well on the swim, bike, and/or run, but take too much time in transition. Lay out your clothes and try practicing in your backyard with a timer. Here are the steps to make transitions easier and more efficient.

1. Put a towel down or a transition mat.
2. Place your running shoes (sneakers) on the back of the towel or transition mat, ensuring your laces are open.
3. Put your running belt or hydration belt on top of your sneakers.
4. Then, place your running cap or visor upside down on top of your sneakers so that you can put it on quickly.
5. Place your bike shoes or towel (if you are wearing clip-ons) at the front of the mat and ensure they are fully open.
6. Put your helmet on top of your bike shoes. (Some people clip their helmets to the bike handlebars, but I always put mine down on my shoes, just in case someone bumps into my bike during the transition, so the helmet doesn't get damaged.)
7. Lastly, place your sunglasses open inside your helmet.
8. Finally, if you need a gel or a bottle of water, place it on the side of the transition.

When you are in transition, ensure the hydration bottles are on the bike. If you wear a hydration belt during the run, ensure it has the bottles securely in place.

Listen to Your Body

While pushing yourself is important, listening to your body is equally crucial. Rest when you need to, and don't ignore any signs of injury. The goal is to compete in a triathlon and enjoy the training journey.

QUICK TIPS

- Practice transitions and brick workouts.
- Stick to a training plan and complete all the workouts, even if you don't feel like it.
- Hire a coach if you need individualized help.
- Listen to your body and take a rest day if you need it.

CHAPTER 37

Balancing Triathlon Training With Life

"While participating in my first triathlon, I never took off my wetsuit and rode my bike 12 miles in a full wetsuit." –Pathetic Triathlete Member

Triathlon training, whether for a sprint, Olympic, half-distance, or full-distance event, is a commitment that requires dedication, discipline, and time. Juggling this rigorous training schedule with work, family responsibilities, and other aspects of life can be challenging. However, it's not impossible. You can balance your triathlon training with your daily life with the right strategies.

First, prioritize your tasks and plan your day, week, or even month. Think about what is important in your life and what can be put on hold during your training. Make a schedule that includes your workout sessions, work commitments, family time, and rest periods. This will provide you with a clear understanding of how to allocate your time effectively and efficiently.

Train smarter, not harder. Incorporate HIIT (High-Intensity Interval Training) into your regimen to get maximum results quickly. To save time, consider combining workouts, such as a bike ride followed by a short run. The goal is not to spend endless hours training but to train effectively.

You don't have to do everything yourself. Share household chores and responsibilities with your partner, children, or roommates. Outsource tasks such as cleaning, grocery shopping, or other errands. This will free up more of your time for training and recovery.

Use downtime wisely. If you're watching television, stretch or do light-strengthening exercises. If you're stuck in a waiting room, read up on strategies to improve your performance.

Getting your workout done first thing in the morning can help prevent it from being pushed aside later when unexpected tasks or commitments arise. Plus, it leaves your evenings free to spend time with family or relax.

Involve your family in your training whenever possible. Go for bike rides or runs with your partner or children. This will help you stay fit and provide quality family time. When I first started running, I would take my kids to the local track and play games with them. We would play, "Who can outrun Mom?" or "Who can go the furthest without stopping?" or "Who can run to the flagpole the fastest?" This made me feel so good.

Even today, despite my children being adults, I still include them in running races. I am so happy when I run a race with either my son or daughter or both!

Rest is just as important as training. Schedule rest days into your regimen to allow your body to recover and prevent burnout.

"Balancing being a mother of four, working full time, and training for Ironman races means prioritizing what truly matters: my family, job, and workouts. I make time for my training where I can, let go of stressing over undone chores, and accept that sacrifices, such as social time, are part of the journey. It's not about having it all perfectly done, but about passionately pursuing what I love and cherishing what is most important," said Leah Jantzen, Triathlete and Kona 2022 finisher.

Balancing triathlon training with life's responsibilities may sometimes seem overwhelming, but remember your why. You can manage it all with careful planning, efficient training, and a supportive network.

QUICK TIPS

- Review your schedule and establish your priorities. Reschedule something if you can.
- Prioritize triathlon training in the morning. Then, you can focus on family and work responsibilities during the day.

CHAPTER 38

How to Train in Inclement Weather

"I once ran the wrong way out of transition for a 70.3 and added an extra 1.5 miles or so to my day before I figured it out." –WeREndurance Member

Adaptability is the key to triathlon training and racing. On race day, you have no control over the weather. It could be sunny and calm, windy, pouring rain, or blisteringly hot. Therefore, it is important to prepare for all possible conditions during your training, including inclement weather.

When I signed up for Ironman New York in 2023, I was so psyched to get it done. I put in hours of training, and the weather was perfect on the packet pickup day. But on the race day, it was a nor'easter with 30 mph winds and heavy rain. Although the race went forward as planned, I called off the race for myself that morning. As the race continued, the race director kept shortening it so that more people would finish, but it was still hazardous. And, for me, I felt it was unsafe. (Although I did have FOMO after looking at everyone's photos on Facebook.)

Open-water Swim

Training for an open-water swim in adverse weather can be challenging, but it's not impossible. When the weather is rough or if there is a threat of lightning, head to an indoor pool. This will enable you to maintain your training rhythm.

If the weather conditions are manageable, an open-water swim could be good. Swimming in choppy waters or under a gray sky will help you gain confidence and learn to adapt your techniques to the conditions. Safety is imperative. Always have a buddy system or lifeguard present. As noted in chapter 18, ensure you wear a portable buoy so you can be seen.

Cycling Nor'easter

Cycling in adverse weather can be dangerous due to slippery roads and reduced visibility. One option is to use a stationary bike or an indoor trainer.

This allows you to work on your cadence, power, and endurance regardless of the weather outside.

If you choose to cycle outdoors, invest in proper gear. Waterproof jackets, thermal layers, gloves, and shoe covers can make wet or cold rides more tolerable. Also, ensure your bike is equipped with lights and reflectors for visibility. Always prioritize safety; if conditions are too severe, switching to an indoor workout is a better option.

Road Surface Conditions

Wet or icy roads significantly reduce your bike's traction, making it easier to lose control. Avoid riding over painted road markings, such as pedestrian crossings or lane dividers, as they can be incredibly slippery when wet. Similarly, metal surfaces, such as manhole covers or railway tracks, can be treacherously slick in the rain.

Puddles can also be dangerous, as they conceal potholes or other road irregularities. Try to avoid them when possible, but if you must ride through one, do so straight and avoid sudden turns or braking.

Grates and Bridges

Drain grates, particularly those with bars parallel to your direction of travel, can catch your wheels and cause accidents. Always avoid these when riding, especially in poor weather when visibility might be reduced.

Bridges can present challenges. In cold weather, they freeze before the rest of the road, creating icy patches. In rainy conditions, water runoff can make them more slippery than other parts of the road. Use caution when crossing bridges, reduce speed, and avoid sudden maneuvers.

Leaves and Debris

Wet leaves can be as slick as ice, and large piles of leaves can hide other hazards. Similarly, high winds during storms can leave debris scattered across the road, posing a risk on your ride.

Braking Distance

Avoid sudden stops, and give yourself plenty of room to slow down or stop.

If you decide to cycle in inclement weather, be aware of potential hazards. Safety should be your top priority. If conditions are too hazardous, consider postponing your ride or opting for an indoor training session.

Running

Running is the most weather-resistant discipline in triathlon. Rain or shine, hot or cold, you can usually find a way to get your run in. If it's raining, dress appropriately with water-resistant clothing and shoes with a good grip. You may even consider wearing trail shoes. If it's cold, layer up and pay attention to extremities like your hands and ears, which can get particularly cold.

Running on a treadmill is also an option during severe weather. While it doesn't perfectly mimic outdoor running, you can adjust the incline to simulate hills and control your pace more accurately.

Mental Preparation

Lastly, a significant part of dealing with inclement weather is mental. It's about having the toughness to push through uncomfortable conditions. Use bad weather training days as opportunities to strengthen your mental resilience. Visualize your success in overcoming the weather challenge to apply this mindset on race day.

You can't control the weather on race day. However, you can control how you prepare for it. If you train smart and equip yourself with the right gear, you will be set up for success at your next race. Consider inclement weather as an opportunity to prove your resilience and determination as a triathlete.

QUICK TIPS

- If it's raining, don't fret. Go outside and get it done.
- If the weather is extreme, remember there is always an indoor option.
- If the weather is bad on race day, you may want to opt out of the race. Go with your comfort level. If you feel the weather is not that bad, then race.
- Don't let the weather be an excuse for you not to train or race.

Jodie Robertson
Professional Triathlete, Melville, NY

Before I started competing in triathlons, I had a running background. I ran a lot. But I was going through a continuous cycle of getting injured, recovering, running, and then getting injured again. My only cycling experience came from riding a "rinky dinky" bike I used to ride with a friend.

One day, I told him jokingly, "I'm going to be a pro-triathlete."

He said, "How can that happen? You can't even swim."

I was half-kidding but also serious. The allure of the challenge was there, and I was intrigued.

I raced cross-country in the 2012 Olympic Marathon Trials and didn't make it. In the summer of 2014, I wanted to qualify for the 2016 trials, but I kept getting injured.

So, I signed up for Ironman Lake Placid. I spent over $800 to sign up because I didn't want to keep running 120 to 140 miles a week and risk getting injured. Instead, I learned to swim and rode my bike more often. I switched up my training. Instead of running 140 miles a week, I started running 70 miles a week and incorporated swimming and biking into my training regimen.

I raced a marathon and ran a 5:54/mile pace that fall. I qualified for the 2016 Olympic Trials and was thrilled that I didn't have to run those 140 miles per week. The cross-training had helped. I finished fourth at the 2015 US Marathon Championships.

After this, I switched gears and signed up for Quassy 70.3 and Syracuse 70.3. They were two weeks apart. I thought I should try a triathlon before the Lake Placid event.

I felt like I had so much endurance.

I bought a triathlon bike with a power meter and hired a triathlon coach who gave me swim, bike and run workouts. Then, I signed up for Quassy.

When the big day came, I noticed a woman who was around my age who was an excellent cyclist. I knew she would be my competition.

Quassy had a lake swim. It was uneventful. However, it was my first time wearing a race kit and a wetsuit. The swim was done in small age group waves. I felt like I was by myself. I knew I was a slow swimmer, but there was no pressure.

I'm sure I took my time in transition. Then I jumped on the bike. It was a hilly course. (I was happy that I rode the course ahead of time with a friend. Knowing the course was helpful.)

But then, during the run, I passed the Boston competitor. I ran a 1:22 on the half marathon. I even stopped on the run to go to the bathroom.

I won Quassy, and then a few weeks later, I also won Syracuse Ironman with a time of 4:38:21.

Unfortunately, that same year, I was riding my bike and got hit by a car in my neighborhood, broke my clavicle, and didn't race Lake Placid.

While recovering, I investigated getting my pro card and hired a new coach. Then, there were new criteria, but I got my pro card by competing in Quassy and Syracuse.

In March 2016, I started racing as a pro.

CHAPTER 39

Strength Training for Triathletes

"Once I signed up for a race, I duly put it on the calendar and started training. Watching TV a week before the race, saw some media coverage showing highlights from the race. Yep, it was a DNS because I put it on the calendar for the wrong day." –Pathetic Triathlete Member

Strength training is a crucial component of triathlon training. Strength training enhances power, prevents injury, and promotes overall athletic performance. Although many of us dislike strength training, it's important. Work it into your schedule by completing at least two weekly sessions, each lasting 30 minutes. During the off-season, try to do at least three 30-minute to 1-hour weekly sessions.

"The key here is to slow it down," said Sharon Levy, MSPT, Co-Owner of Excel Physical Therapy and Workout. "Avoid using momentum. Aim for controlled motions to activate the targeted muscles optimally."

Core strength is crucial for all three disciplines of a triathlon. A strong core improves your swimming technique by enabling better rotation and stability in the water. On the bike, it helps maintain an efficient cycling posture, reducing fatigue. A strong core keeps your form solid during the run, especially when fatigue sets in during the race's later stages. Exercises such as planks, bridges, and Russian twists are excellent for building core strength.

The lower body, including the gluteal muscles, quadriceps, hamstrings, and calves, plays a significant role in activities such as cycling, running, and swimming. Strengthening these muscles can improve your pedaling power and running stride. Squats, lunges, deadlifts, calf raises, and hamstring curls are beneficial exercises for the lower body.

While less critical than core and lower-body strength, upper-body strength is important for the swim portion of a triathlon. Strong shoulders, back, and arm muscles can enhance your swim stroke and endurance in the water. Pull-ups, push-ups, lat pulldowns, and rows can help strengthen these areas.

Balancing strength training with your other workouts is all about smart scheduling. Here are some strategies:

- You can combine your strength and endurance workouts on the same day. For example, you might run in the morning and do a strength workout in the evening.
- Fit in a brief strength workout after a hard run, bike ride, or swim session.
- Focus more on strength training in the off-season when the volume of swim, bike, and run workouts is lower.
- Allow rest days between intense workouts to give your body time to recover and adapt.

Strength Training Routine

Each strength training session should include core, lower, and upper-body body. The best place to start is YouTube or Dynamic Triathlete, where you can find various strength training routines for triathletes.

Start with lighter weights and focus on proper form. As you get stronger, gradually increase the weight or resistance to continue challenging your muscles.

Periodization

Like your overall triathlon training, your strength training should be periodized, meaning it should vary throughout your training cycle. In the base phase of training, focus on building overall strength. As you approach your race, incorporate more plyometric exercises to shift the focus to power and speed. Plyometrics, or "jump training," involves explosive movements like jumps, hops, and bounds. Think of activities like jump squats or even clapping push-ups.

Strength training is important–balance it with your swimming, biking, and running. Always listen to your body and allow ample time for recovery to avoid overtraining.

Strength training is a tool that can improve performance and injury prevention in triathlon. Incorporating a well-rounded strength training routine into your schedule will set the stage for a more robust, efficient, and successful race.

In addition to strength training, try balancing on one leg at a time to improve ankle stability and engage your core. Buy a balance board on Amazon for core strength and work on it daily for 3–5 minutes. (Believe me, this is hard but important to do.)

QUICK TIPS

- Make sure to incorporate strength into your training plan. You should strength train twice a week for 30 minutes at a minimum.
- Start easy and build up. You will notice the difference that strength training makes in your triathlon training.

CHAPTER 40

Preparing for Triathlon Race Day

"I walked up to the transition body marker to get marked. I said, 'My age is 26.' The marker wrote my age on one arm and turned to the other arm. The marker asked, 'And what's your race?' Confused, I responded, 'Huh?' The marker repeated, 'Race.' Still not getting it, I said, 'My race?' The marker clarified, 'Yeah, like, what race are you?' I hesitated, 'Uuuh, white? Caucasian?' The marker gave me a bewildered look and said, 'No, like what RACE are you?' Finally understanding, I replied, 'Ooooooohhhhh. Long Course.' The marker marked me, and we parted ways in very awkward silence." –Pathetic Triathlete Member

The excitement of a triathlon race day can be tinged with anxiety, especially when it comes to ensuring you have everything you need. I'm always nervous before a race. I have a checklist of everything I bring, and I am still anxious. Recently, I competed in a race in St. Petersburg. I flew to Tampa from New York and thought I had everything I needed, but of course, I forgot my socks! Thankfully, at packet pickup, I could purchase socks but couldn't get the ones I like to wear during training.

Although I had a checklist, I still forgot something—my advice: double-check your list. A race checklist is included in the back of the book, but below is what you should and should not bring to a race.

At Packet Pickup

When race weekend is finally here, after 12–20 weeks of preparation, it's time to pick up your packet. Inside, you will get a swim cap with the color of your race wave (your swim start). You will also get a race number. There will be the same number for your bike and bike helmet. You will have to wear the race bib during the run portion of the triathlon. In addition, you may also get race tattoos. Each race is different, but most will require you to place the race number on your arm and leg. There are also some races where you must put your age on the back of your leg. Since this isn't a mandatory requirement for the USAT, many races have been opting out of including this. But there are still some race companies that do. So, you should wear it, even if you don't want to.

The age on your leg means you know who your competition is on the course. Most races have awards based on four- to five-year age groups. So, if you are 37, you will race with the 35- to 40-year-olds. If you are 61, you will compete against the 60–64 age group.

At the packet pickup, you may be told to rack your bike. You do this by attaching the seat to the post. You can leave your bike overnight. It will be secure, and the race company will have guards to watch your items. Don't leave anything other than your bike in transition before the race. Some local races may have you rack your bike on race morning.

If you have electric shifters, charge your bike the night before the race. I once forgot to do this, and my gears wouldn't shift on race day. I will never forget to do this again.

What to Wear to the Triathlon

Wear your tri kit to the triathlon. Wear socks, if you use them, along with your sneakers. Additionally, you may want to wear your cap or visor, as well as your prescription lenses or sunglasses. Before you get to the race site, douse yourself with anti-chafing cream. Put it on your neck, under your arms, between your toes, and anywhere else that can get chafed. Also, don't forget to wear sunscreen. It may be dark when you get to transition, but the bike and run portions will be during the heat of the day.

What to Bring to a Triathlon

Put everything in a transition bag. This is a bag large enough to hold all your gear. My first mistake was bringing several bags, each containing various items. I quickly learned that this isn't ideal. You need one bag to carry everything. Also, bring as little as possible. Only bring the essentials, including the following:

For the swim

- Wetsuit.
- Goggles and an extra pair in case they break.
- Race swim cap (this will be given to you by the race company at packet pickup).

- Earplugs or nose plugs, if you wear them.
- Anti-chafing balm.
- A small towel to dry off before the bike stage (you can also use this as a transition mat).

For the bike

- Your bike (if you haven't racked it the night before). Make sure your number is visible on the bike.
- Helmet with your number on it (which will be given to you at packet pickup).
- Sunglasses.
- Cycling shoes.
- A spare tire tube and a CO_2 cartridge or mini pump are also useful for emergencies. (Put these in a utility bag on the bike.)

Run gear

- Running shoes.
- Socks.
- Hat or visor.
- Gymboss timer (if you are doing run/walk intervals).
- Race belt with your race number attached.

Miscellaneous things to bring

- Nutrition and Hydration—Energy gels, bars, electrolyte tablets, and water bottles. Stick with what you've tested in training.

- Other Essentials—Sunscreen, lip balm, insect repellent, a first aid kit, a multi-tool for bike adjustments, and extra safety pins. If it rains or there is a threat of rain, get a dry bag and put your stuff in it.

Setting Up Transition

In your transition area, you switch from swimming to cycling gear (T1) and cycling to running gear (T2). Set up your transition area efficiently.

Find your assigned spot and rack your bike by the saddle. Place the saddle over the rack and ensure it is secure so it won't easily tip over.

After you do that, look around you. Where is the swim-in (this is where you will be running into transition from the swim), bike-in, bike-out, and run-out? The run-in is the finish line. Count the rows for each and remember them. Also, memorize your race number. You don't want to be all frazzled on race morning. This will help you be as organized as possible.

Lay out your gear. Place your helmet on your handlebars with the straps open, or leave it on your cycling shoes on the ground for a quick transition. I prefer keeping it on the ground in case someone bumps into my bike; I don't have to worry that it will fall.

Arrange your cycling shoes, socks (if you're wearing them), sunglasses, and any nutrition you plan to take on the bike. If you are wearing cycling shoes, keep them open. You may want to put baby powder inside them after the swim. (An experienced triathlete may even clip the shoes on the bike. They will run out of transition barefoot and then put on their shoes while cycling.)

Lay out your running shoes and hat or visor behind your bike gear. Ensure your race number is visible on your belt to exit the transition area quickly. Also, make sure your sneakers are unlaced.

To respect other athletes' areas, keep your gear within your allotted space. It should be under the front wheel off the ground.

What NOT to Bring

- A balloon or a marker to mark your spot.
- A bucket with water to soak your feet after the swim.
- New gear or nutrition you have yet to test in training. Race day is not the time to try something new that could cause discomfort or digestive issues.
- Valuable items or anything you don't need for the race.
- Headphones or earbuds, unless you only want them for transition. They are not allowed on the swim, bike, or run course.

Preparing for race day involves careful planning and organization. Because each triathlete has unique needs and preferences, tailor this guide to your requirements. You got this!

QUICK TIPS

- To transition, bring as little as you can. The more you bring, the more disorganized you will become.
- Don't mark your spot. It's not legal in triathlon. Don't bring a balloon or a tie. Instead, make a mental note of where the bike is racked. You can bring a colorful towel or a transition mat to put your stuff on.

CHAPTER 41

Mental Training

"I got halfway through a very long drive to a triathlon when I reached through my shirt to rub my sore shoulder and realized I had forgotten to wear my sports bra. Instead, I wore my old, worn-out, flimsy, zero-elasticity, underwire satin bra. And I'm what you would call 'chesty.' As I changed into my tri suit in the car upon arrival, I crisscrossed the bra straps, which gave the illusion of sportiness but none of the support. It was an obscene sight, and I felt bad for all the young people who must surely be scarred for life from having had to see me running and bouncing along." –Pathetic Triathlete Member

It's natural to compare yourself to others instead of just looking at yourself. Friendly competition is always good, but not when it makes you feel bad.

It can be difficult not to compare yourself to others on Strava, but try not to get bogged down in comparison. Focus on yourself.

While physical training is the cornerstone of triathlon preparation, mental training should be considered. A strong mind can be as crucial as a strong body when pushing your limits in a triathlon.

Triathlons are grueling. They test your endurance, strength, and resilience, both physically and mentally. Mental training helps build confidence, maintain focus, manage stress, and overcome setbacks. It can distinguish between giving up mid-race and crossing the finish line.

Mental toughness refers to your ability to perform consistently under pressure and adversity. It's about maintaining determination, focus, and confidence despite your challenges. Here are some strategies to build your mental toughness:

- Visualizing your race from start to finish can help prepare your mind for the event. Imagine every detail—the pre-race nerves, the adrenaline rush at the beginning, the fatigue during the race, and the exhilaration of crossing the finish line. Visualization can help reduce anxiety and increase confidence. I had a friend who was a coach, and he used to say to me, "Walk me through your triathlon from the beginning of the swim, through transitions, on the bike, back in transition, and to the run. What does it feel like to finish the race?"
- Setting specific, measurable, achievable, relevant, and time-bound (SMART) goals can provide motivation and a sense of direction. Goals give you something to strive for and allow you to measure your progress. An example would be, "I will make it to the pool today and swim what

my coach tells me to swim, no matter how long it takes." Or, during the race, say to yourself, "I will complete this race no matter how hard or how long it feels."

- The way you talk to yourself greatly influences your performance. Positive self-talk can boost your confidence and help you push through tough moments. Phrases like "I can do this" or "I am strong" can make a significant difference. I constantly coach myself during training and racing. I say things like, "I got this," and "We can do this."
- Mindfulness involves being fully present in the moment and aware of where you are and what you're doing. It's a powerful tool for managing stress and improving focus. You can practice mindfulness during your training, focusing on your breath, the rhythm of your stride, or the sensation of your feet hitting the ground. When you race in a triathlon, you stay focused on the moment. Stay in the swim, bike, and run. Don't think, "What's next?" Focus on the here and now.
- Meditation can help clear your mind and reduce anxiety. Regular practice can enhance your focus and mental clarity, enabling you to better handle the pressures of race day.
- Pre-race nerves can be overwhelming. Establishing a pre-race routine can help manage this anxiety. This routine may involve visualization, deep breathing exercises, listening to motivating music, or completing a checklist for the race.
- Consider bringing your earbuds to listen to relaxing music before the race. Many people are anxious, and their anxiety can rub off on you. However, if you do bring earbuds, leave them at the transition site before the swim. You cannot use personal devices during the event.

Mental training is a vital component of triathlon preparation. Incorporating mental training strategies into your routine can enhance your performance and overall triathlon experience. The mind is a powerful tool—train it well, and it will serve you well on race day and beyond.

QUICK TIPS

- Use visualization. Imagine yourself in the race: from the start to T1, then on the bike to T2, and finally, on the run to the finish line.
- Try meditating or listening to music to calm your nerves. Take a deep breath, and remember: You got this!

Jackie Miller
Triathlon Coach with QT2, Sarasota, Florida

Born and raised in Ohio, I was an active child who dabbled in soccer, basketball, and track. However, after moving to Florida in the 9th grade, I discovered that there were no girls' soccer teams, which forced me to join a boys' team. I eventually quit soccer and continued with track until the 11th grade.

Staying fit was important to me throughout high school, college, and my early working years, and I religiously hit the gym after work. Life took a turn when I had three children, and I wanted to shed the extra weight I'd gained during this period.

We were getting our pool repaired at the time, and the serviceman looked remarkably fit. I asked about his fitness regimen, and he recommended his trainer at Gold's Gym. Intriguingly, this trainer also happened to be a triathlon coach, and he suggested I try competing in a triathlon.

Initially, I chuckled at the idea.

My next-door neighbor, a triathlete, offered to sell me her triathlon bike for $500. Since I was planning a girls' trip, I decided to think about the offer upon my return. During the trip, I saved money instead of spending it on non-essentials.

When I returned home, I impulsively bought the bike, even before committing to a triathlon.

Soon thereafter, I contacted my trainer and signed up for his coaching almost four to six months before my first sprint triathlon. At the time, I was in my 30s.

My first "brick" training session was tough, but soon everything began to fall into place.

During my first swimming session, I realized I knew nothing about swimming. I arrived without goggles, my long hair untied, and wearing a tankini. I struggled to make it to the end of the pool, and my coach remarked that we had a lot of work ahead.

I initially swam with my head above water, and when I did submerge, I held my breath. An elderly man at the pool noticed my struggle and taught me how to breathe underwater. My coach and I spent weeks blowing bubbles and learning proper breathing techniques.

Cycling was a breeze on the flat Florida terrain, and I felt confident on the bike and during the run.

My first sprint took place on Siesta Key, organized by the local Sarasota swim team. The event included an 800-meter swim, a 13-mile bike ride, and a 5K run on the sand, which proved challenging.

The other athletes intimidated me when I swam in the choppy Gulf of Mexico, but I managed to get through it.

I remember my heart pounding as I raced through the sand, cheered on by my kids holding "Go, Mommy" signs. Despite the challenges, I loved the experience.

Interestingly, my triathlon coach, who was initially my trainer, later became my business partner in our coaching venture. We now jointly coach for QT2. It's fascinating how life comes full circle.

CHAPTER 42

How to Embrace Outcomes

"At ITU Worlds in 2008, it was so cold that they canceled the swim AFTER the age groupers started. Almost everyone was hypothermic at the finish. I could not feel my feet or hands. I was DFL (Dead F-in Last) or near DFL and was rushed into the med tent to warm up - stripped down and given a blanket, that's it. If it weren't Worlds, I would have quit." –Pathetic Triathlete Member

Taking the first step to sign up for and race a triathlon speaks volumes about your courage, determination, and spirit of adventure. However, as with any challenging pursuit, only some stories written on the racecourse have a finish-line photo.

In triathlon, terms like DNF (Did Not Finish), DNS (Did Not Start), and DQ (Disqualified) represent outcomes that are a part of many athletes' journeys. It's not a bad thing. Sometimes, things out of our control happen. While they may initially feel like setbacks, they hold important lessons and opportunities for growth.

DNF (Did Not Finish)

DNF is a notation in race results indicating an athlete who started the race but did not finish. There are many reasons why an athlete might not finish a race, from physical injury to mechanical failures, such as your bike breaking down. It's crucial to remember that choosing to listen to your body and prioritize your well-being is a sign of strength, not weakness.

If you've ever experienced a DNF, know it doesn't define your capability or diminish your effort. Given the day's circumstances, you showed up, started, and gave it your all. That courage to try and push your limits already sets you apart. Remember, every champion has faced setbacks; what matters is the resilience to come back stronger. DNF is not a bad word. It happens to the best of us.

DNS (Did Not Start)

DNS indicates an athlete who did not start the race. This can be due to injury, illness, personal emergencies, or pre-race nerves. Deciding not to start, especially after months of training, can be a brutal decision. Yet, it's a testament to an athlete's maturity and self-awareness to recognize when it's not the right time to race.

When I signed up for the Half Ironman in Jones Beach, I pulled myself out of the race before I started. The forecast called for a torrential rainstorm and a tropical storm. I felt it was unsafe. As the race director didn't call off the race, I decided I would not put myself through that, especially on the bike course.

If you've encountered a DNS, it's okay to feel disappointed, but also be proud of yourself for making a tough decision that was best for you at that moment. The journey to the start line is filled with lessons, growth, and accomplishments that remain valuable, regardless of whether the race begins.

DQ (Disqualified)

Being disqualified, or DQ'd, means an athlete has violated a rule of the race. Common reasons include drafting in non-draft-legal races, not completing the full course, or failing to serve penalty time. Sometimes, you may have yet to learn that something you did was against the rules. While it can be disheartening, being DQ'd offers a learning opportunity to understand race rules better and improve your strategy for future competitions.

It's important to approach a DQ with a mindset focused on growth. Reflect on the mistake, learn from it, and use the experience to become a more knowledgeable and skilled athlete.

Experiencing a DNF, DNS, or DQ can be tough, but it's part of the journey in the sport of triathlon—a journey that only a fraction of people dare to embark on. It could have been your training, or it could have been something that you had no control over.

Less than 1% of the world's population is estimated to have completed a triathlon. You've accomplished something extraordinary by standing at the start line or committing to train.

These outcomes do not signify failure; they are stepping stones on your path as an athlete. They teach resilience, humility, and perseverance. They remind us that the true essence of triathlon is not just about finishing races but about embracing challenges, celebrating progress, and continually striving to be our best selves.

So, if you've faced a DNF, DNS, or DQ, remember that you tried, and in trying, you did more than those who never dared to step out of their comfort zones. Your journey is unique, filled with its highs and lows, and every step, every decision, and every outcome is a testament to your courage and dedication. Keep moving forward, for the true victory in triathlon lies in the journey, the community, and the endless pursuit of personal excellence.

QUICK TIPS

- Don't get down on yourself for not finishing a race. There is always a reason why. Understand the reason and move on.
- If you DNS, it's okay. You are awesome for training and doing your best under the circumstances.

CHAPTER 43

Post-Race Recovery Strategies

"IMCA 2023, torrential rain began as I started the second loop on the bike. Stopped at an aid station to use the porta-potty, and I, along with eight other athletes, ended up with buckets of mud in our cleats. Two volunteers attempted to clean our shoes, but I gave up waiting and proceeded with just one shoe clipped in. I stopped at the next aid station about 5 miles down the road, on the return side, and a talented volunteer cleaned my other cleat, so I was able to clip back in. From that point forward, I didn't stop at any aid stations—it was pouring, so I taught myself how to pee on the bike and did so for the rest of the race. (Including on the run, which was also torrential rain)!" –Pathetic Triathlete Member

Recovering from a triathlon or any endurance race is as important as the training leading up to it. Proper recovery allows your body to heal and adapt to the stress of the race, setting you up for better performance in the future.

Finishing my first official 70.3 Aqua Bike at the Mightyman Montauk in 2024, Montauk, NY.

Here are some tips and strategies to aid your post-race recovery:

- Cool down with a short, gentle jog or walk that helps flush out lactic acid buildup in your muscles and speeds up recovery. Many people skip this step, but it's essential because it reduces the risk of injury and improves flexibility.
- Hydration and refueling are crucial. As soon as the race is over, replenish your body's depleted nutrients. Drink water or sports drinks to rehydrate and replace lost electrolytes. Consume a balanced meal with a good mix of carbohydrates and protein to kick-start recovery.
- Heat and vibration can have varied effects on the body, largely

dependent on their frequency (the rate of vibration) and amplitude (the intensity of vibration). One of my tools is an old-fashioned heating pad. This helps to circulate blood and aids in recovery. Another example is the MyoStorm Meteor, a ball that uses heat and vibration. It has been shown to enhance blood flow, alleviate muscle stiffness, reduce pain perception, and stimulate the nervous system to prompt quicker healing responses within the body. This powerful combination of effects accelerates the healing process for injuries and aches while maintaining flexibility and preventing potential injuries.

- Ice baths or cold plunges are popular recovery methods among athletes due to their effectiveness in reducing muscle soreness and accelerating recovery. They reduce inflammation, limit swelling, stimulate the nervous system, and release endorphins, the body's natural painkillers. These endorphins provide a natural high and further reduce the perception of post-workout pain. They also enhance mental resilience.
- Rest is crucial after a race. Your body needs time to repair and rebuild damaged muscle tissue. Allow yourself a few days of rest or more, depending on the race distance. Sleep is when most of the body's repair work happens. Ensure you get plenty of quality sleep in the days following the race.
- Active recovery involves engaging in low-intensity, low-impact exercise on your rest days, rather than taking complete rest. It's all about moving your body gently to stimulate blood flow without straining your muscles. This type of movement helps accelerate the recovery process by reducing muscle stiffness and soreness, promoting circulation, and flushing out toxins. Examples include walking, yoga, or a light bike ride.
- Maintain a balanced diet. Continue eating a diet rich in lean proteins, fruits, vegetables, and whole grains to give your body the necessary nutrients for recovery.
- Stay hydrated in the days following the race to help maintain optimal bodily function and promote healing.

- Further, a warm bath can be incredibly soothing for tired muscles. I like to use products with Epsom salt, which is believed to help relax muscles and loosen stiff joints. Pour a generous amount into warm water and soak for at least 15 minutes. The magnesium in Epsom salts can help reduce inflammation, while the warm water aids circulation and soothes sore muscles.
- Lastly, everyone's recovery rate is different. Listen to your body and give it the rest it needs. If you're feeling excessively tired, experiencing prolonged muscle soreness, or having trouble sleeping, consider consulting a healthcare professional.

QUICK TIPS

- Take advantage of your recovery. Enjoy it.
- Don't come back too soon. Take your time and recover fully before starting training again.

CHAPTER 44

Off-Season Training and Cross-Training Strategies

"Was doing a reverse triathlon. I came in from the bike and took off for the swim. Completed it and came back into transition and discovered someone had thrown up all over my open tri bag (and some of my gear). The trash can was on the other side of my bike. Someone must have had a rough race! I had to get a new bag!" –Pathetic Triathlete Member

The off-season, the period following your last race of the year, is critical for rest, recovery, and preparation for the upcoming season. This offers an opportunity to recharge physically and mentally while maintaining fitness and working on areas of weakness. Even if you live in a place with good weather all year, you should take a few weeks off before signing up for your next race.

After the season's final race, giving your body a break from the rigors of training is essential. The length of this rest period can vary depending on factors like your overall health, the intensity of your past season, and your goals for the next season. However, a general rule of thumb is to take about two weeks completely off from structured training. This doesn't mean total inactivity; light activities, such as walking or easy cycling, are fine and can even aid recovery.

Once you've had some downtime, it's important to maintain a base level of fitness. Focus on moderate, consistent exercise to keep your cardiorespiratory system in shape and muscles engaged.

The off-season is the perfect time to incorporate cross-training into your routine. Cross-training refers to training in disciplines other than your primary sport to improve overall performance.

In the winter, try skiing, snowboarding, or snowshoeing. You can also try an indoor activity, such as basketball or hockey. These are excellent ways to cross-train.

Strength training is another excellent cross-training option. As I mentioned in chapter 39, aim for at least three 30-minute or longer weekly sessions. Focused resistance workouts can improve your power, stability, and resilience, leading to better performance and injury prevention.

Use the off-season to work on specific skills or areas of weakness. For example, you could improve your swimming technique, cycling efficiency, or running form.

The off-season is about physical recovery and mental rest. Taking a break from the intensity and structure of in-season training can help prevent burnout and keep your passion for the sport alive. Engage in other hobbies, spend time with loved ones, and allow yourself some flexibility in your training schedule.

Ultimately, the off-season is an ideal time to begin planning for the upcoming season. Reflect on the past season, identify areas for improvement, set goals for the upcoming season, and start building a training plan.

QUICK TIPS

- Take a break from triathlon training and do something different if you want. Try skiing, snowboarding, or hiking to stay active in winter. This will make it easy when you return to triathlon training.
- Focus on areas you need improvement, such as strength training.

Megan White
Triathlete, Queens, NY

I was an adult-onset athlete. I never participated in organized high school sports. In high school, I opted for running as my gym activity. We had to run around the Jerome Park Reservoir by Lehman College in the Bronx. But that was that.

As an adult who wanted to get in shape, I occasionally went to the track and gym. I loved the water and always admired people swimming laps. Watching them swim back and forth looked awesome, and I wanted to learn how to do that.

So, I joined a beginner swim class at the Y, which was a few stops from where I worked. They started by having us put our faces in the water. Since I had passed that point, I joined the Beginner II program.

I was in the slower section with some older people. In the third or fourth week, the instructor asked, "How many are training for the

NYC Tri this summer?" Most of the class raised their hands. I looked around and thought, "How will these people do a triathlon? They don't swim much better than me."

While talking with an older woman in my lane, I said, "I can't believe these people are doing a triathlon."

She replied, "You've never done a triathlon? There's one on Long Island for women. You would absolutely love it."

I told her it wasn't my thing and that they were all "delusional." But curiosity got the best of me, and I looked it up to see if I could do it.

Months later, I signed up for the Danskin Triathlon for women at the Aquatic Center at Eisenhower Park. It was funny at the event; I got a tap on the shoulder. "I knew you would do this. You're going to have a great time," said the older woman from the Y.

Before I crossed the finish line, I was hooked. I loved it. I stayed long after I finished, cheering others on. I was on fire and completely hooked.

I placed in the first Danskin Triathlon in 2009. They held a seminar to explain what we needed to do for the triathlon. I wore my bathing suit and bike shorts.

After the triathlon, I bought every book about triathlons and followed numerous websites and blogs to learn as much as I could.

I loved my first mini-triathlon. It was amazing. Since then, I've done the NYC Tri, dozens of sprints and Olympic distance races, one half-distance, and five Ironman events.

CHAPTER 45

When Things Go Wrong—Setbacks

"I cornered a turn wrong at the Key West Triathlon and skidded out. I fell off the bike and hit my head. I was completely bloody. When the police officer asked if I was okay, I replied that I was and then returned to my bike. I wanted to finish the race! I went about 10 feet, maybe less, and fell off the bike again. I could tell that the bike was damaged. And, of course, banged my head yet again. All bloody and bruised, I ended up going via ambulance to the hospital." –Pathetic Triathlete Member

Life is a test of endurance, resilience, and the ability to turn setbacks into comebacks. It is like a triathlon: Things can and will go wrong.

I can't tell you how many times I tore my meniscus. I was training for a half Ironman event, and after a 60-mile bike ride, I went out for a run. Within a half mile, I heard a snap, and that was it. I had to end my season and was devastated.

So, what do you do when life throws you a curveball? Do you dwell on the misfortune? Or do you pick yourself up and continue pushing forward?

There is only one option: keep moving forward.

I was at the beginning of the 2018 triathlon season. That April, I had plans to go to St. Anthony's Triathlon in St. Petersburg. Instead, I spent three dreary weeks in the hospital watching my beautiful sister, Lori, slowly fade away.

Lori was having extreme headaches and was told by her doctors that it was nothing, just migraines. She went to the emergency room three times, and they sent her on her way all three times. In the morning, she collapsed. She had just come from the neurologist, who told her that it looked like migraines and nothing more.

Moments after I spoke with her, she collapsed in her apartment. No one could get through to her. Her boyfriend had a neighbor break into her apartment and found her foaming at the mouth. He immediately called an ambulance, but it was too late. She was in a coma.

Lori had a brain aneurysm and a stroke. She spent three weeks in the hospital in a coma. She passed thereafter. It was one of the most, if not the most, difficult times for me. She was my best friend and my only sister.

After that, I had difficulty training or doing anything related to triathlon. Nothing seemed important anymore.

As time went by, I slowly started to get back. I needed to do something for myself that would clear my head. So, after that, I continued to train and compete until a few months ago, when I, too, was diagnosed with a brain aneurysm. (Apparently, they run in families.)

I started blood thinners in preparation for the elective surgery. I wanted to complete one last triathlon before surgery, so I entered the Key West Triathlon. There, about a mile from T2, I crashed and hit my head twice. I was bleeding all over and had a concussion. Thankfully, the aneurysm didn't rupture. The surgery took place 3 weeks later, and it was a success.

But it did put me back. I struggled to regain shape to compete in 2024 and beyond. Luckily, I found a wonderful coach who helped me get back. As of this publication, I have competed in several running races and returned to St. Petersburg for the St. Anthony's Triathlon. This race is a special significance for me due to both incidents.

So, you can get back, and you will get back.

Training for a triathlon is about physical strength and mental fortitude. It's about harnessing the power of your mind to overcome obstacles, push through pain, and keep going even when every fiber of your being screams at you to stop.

When I underwent brain surgery, I found that my endurance training had prepared me not just physically but mentally as well. Despite the daunting procedure, I recovered faster than expected. My body was used to the rigors of intense training, to the process of breaking down and rebuilding stronger than before. But more importantly, my mind was equipped to handle the challenge.

The discipline, determination, and resilience I had cultivated during my triathlon training became my biggest allies in my recovery journey. I knew how to push through discomfort, stay positive in the face of adversity, and focus on my goal: recovery.

Setbacks are inevitable, but they don't define us. What truly matters is how we respond to these challenges. Whether it's a torn meniscus or brain surgery, these experiences are opportunities to prove to ourselves just how strong we are.

You are built to endure, overcome, and emerge stronger in the face of adversity. Keep pushing forward, training, and proving that no setback is too great to overcome. After all, the greatest victories often come after the most challenging obstacles.

QUICK TIPS

- If something happens to you or a loved one, you will get through it. Triathlon training will help.
- Triathlon training helps you to recover faster from surgery.
- You will get back!

CHAPTER 46

Exploring Alternatives to the Traditional Triathlon

"You learn something new at every race. Sometimes it's that you CAN sweat under a swim cap." –Pathetic Triathlete Member

Triathlons are challenging events that combine swimming, biking, and running. However, not every athlete is drawn to or physically capable of completing all three segments of this demanding race format.

Fortunately, the world of multisport offers a variety of alternatives that cater to different interests and needs. Smaller race companies are at the forefront, offering inclusive events, such as aqua biking, duathlon, and swim/run options. These alternatives provide a fantastic opportunity for athletes to participate in multisport events, even if they have injuries or personal preferences that make a traditional triathlon less appealing.

Aqua Bike

Aqua bike events combine swimming and cycling, eliminating the need for running. This format is ideal for those dealing with impact-related injuries or who prefer not to run. Aqua bike races typically follow the same course as triathlons up to the second transition area, where aqua bike participants finish their race.

This option allows athletes to enjoy the thrill of the swim-to-bike challenge without the strain of running, making it a popular choice for individuals looking to stay active in multisport without the added impact on their joints.

Duathlon

Duathlons offer an engaging alternative for those who prefer to keep their bodies dry. Consisting of a running segment, followed by cycling, and another run, duathlons eliminate the swim component.

This format is perfect for athletes who are strong runners and cyclists but are either uncomfortable in the water or prefer land-based sports. Duathlons vary in distance, ranging from sprint to standard and even longer, more challenging courses, ensuring something for everyone, from beginners to seasoned competitors.

Swim/Run (Aquathlon)

Swim/run events, also known as aquathlons, are a growing segment within the multisport category. These races involve a swimming section followed by a running portion, offering a straightforward, no-transition alternative to traditional triathlons.

The simplicity and focus on just two disciplines make aquathlons an attractive option for newcomers to the sport. Additionally, the absence of a bike leg can make these events more accessible and cost-effective for athletes unwilling or unable to invest in cycling equipment.

The Benefits of Alternatives in the Face of Injury

One of the most significant advantages of these alternative formats is their accessibility to athletes who are recovering from injury. For instance, aqua bike events can be a godsend for runners nursing knee or foot injuries, allowing them to continue competing without exacerbating their condition.

Similarly, duathlons can offer a reprieve for those with shoulder or neck issues that make swimming painful or impossible. Engaging in these alternative events ensures that athletes can maintain their fitness and competitive edge while giving their bodies the time they need to heal properly.

These alternative multisport events can serve as valuable stepping stones for athletes looking to tackle a full triathlon eventually and for athletes nursing injuries. They provide a platform for improving discipline-specific skills and building confidence without the pressure of simultaneously mastering all three triathlon components.

The evolution of multisport into more inclusive and varied events underscores a fundamental truth: anyone can participate in and enjoy the camaraderie and challenge of these competitions. Many smaller race companies offer these options, keeping you feeling like you're in the game.

Recently, I dropped down from a sprint triathlon at the Alpha Win Hudson Valley Triathlon to an aqua bike race instead. To me, it was just as challenging as the run. I'd been dealing with a knee injury that needed surgery, so the run was off the table. However, still participating in the event made me feel great, and I got to challenge myself on some steep hills.

The Relay

In addition to the variety of solo event options available in the multisport arena, relay races represent another exciting and inclusive way to participate in triathlons. Relays bring a team element into what is traditionally seen as an individual endeavor, offering a unique blend of camaraderie, competition, and collective achievement. This format enables athletes of varying strengths and preferences to contribute to a shared goal, making triathlons more accessible to a broader range of participants.

A relay team in a triathlon typically consists of three members (but there can be two), with each person taking on one leg of the race: swimming, biking, or running. This division enables athletes to play to their strengths by focusing on the discipline in which they excel or enjoy the most. It's an excellent option for those who may be exceptionally skilled in one area but less confident or interested in the others.

For example, a strong swimmer who is not as comfortable on the bike or has little interest in running can still experience the thrill and satisfaction of triathlon participation. Similarly, cyclists and runners deterred by the swim portion can participate without venturing into open water.

Accessibility and Team Spirit

Relays open the door to triathlon participation for those who might find the training for all three disciplines daunting due to time constraints, physical limitations, or personal preferences. They also introduce a social aspect to the sport, as teammates support each other through training and racing, celebrating each leg's completion as a step closer to a shared victory.

This team dynamic fosters a sense of belonging and achievement that can be especially appealing to those new to the sport or looking to share the experience with friends or family. The relay format encourages seasoned athletes to mentor newcomers, strengthening the multisport community by bridging the gap between varying levels of experience and ability.

Relays as a Gateway to Full Triathlon Participation

For many, participating in a relay is an introduction to the world of triathlons. It demystifies the sport and provides valuable experience in a supportive environment. Being part of a team can boost confidence and ignite a passion for multisport, eventually encouraging individuals to take on all three disciplines in a solo event.

Other Options

You can focus on a single sport, like a marathon, in addition to a triathlon or any of the other options discussed above.

When I first started, I didn't know that there were single-sport options, such as a 5K swim or a 6.2-mile marathon swim.

Another great thing about this sport is that you can participate in cycling tours, races, mountain biking races, or XTERRA.

For More of a Challenge

An XTERRA race is a unique and challenging multisport event that combines off-road triathlon disciplines. Typically, it encompasses swimming, mountain biking, and trail running. Unlike traditional triathlons, XTERRA pushes athletes to their limits by taking them through rugged natural landscapes.

An XTERRA race consists of:

- Swim–The race begins with an open-water swim, usually in a lake, ocean, or river. Depending on the specific event, the swim course can range from 750 meters to 1.5 kilometers. Swimmers often face unpredictable conditions, such as waves, currents, and varying temperatures, which add to the challenge.
- Mountain Bike–After completing the swim, Participants transition to the mountain biking segment. This portion typically covers 20-40 km through rough terrain, including dirt trails, rocky paths, steep climbs, and thrilling descents. Riders must navigate technical sections that test their bike handling skills and endurance.
- Trail Run–The final leg of an XTERRA race is the trail run, which usually lasts 5-10 kilometers. The route takes runners through forests, streams, and uneven ground. The trail run is designed to be as demanding as the preceding segments, often featuring significant elevation changes and obstacles that require agility and stamina.

What's unique about XTERRA races is that they are set in some of the most beautiful and remote locations, allowing athletes to experience nature up close. The courses are deliberately chosen to highlight the natural beauty and ruggedness of the environment.

UNLOCKING THE TRIATHLON

Whether contending with injuries, navigating personal preferences, or simply looking for a new way to test your endurance, the world of aqua bike, duathlon, swimming/running, relays, and XTERRA offers a welcoming and rewarding avenue for exploration.

The heart of multisport lies not in the specific disciplines themselves but in the spirit of perseverance, community, and personal achievement that binds us all.

QUICK TIPS

- If you are injured, consider an alternative to the triathlon.
- If you feel weak in one area but strong in another, consider an aqua bike, swim/run, duathlon, or relay race.
- If you're starting out, you may consider a relay to get a taste of triathlon.
- Consider an XTERRA race if you are looking for more of a challenge in a beautiful landscape.

PART 6

TRIATHLONS THROUGH YOUR LIFE

People always tell me that they wish they had started younger. Everyone has a reason for starting triathlons when they are ready. I'm glad I started when I did as it allowed me to raise my family and excel in my career. As I got older, I felt I needed a change. This was one of the best changes that happened to me. –Hilary Topper, Author

CHAPTER 47

Triathlons for Kids and Young Adults

"I lost my timing chip in the Hudson River. Not the most pathetic thing, but spending 10 minutes in T1 thinking someone could give me another one was. –Pathetic Triathlete Member

Today, many school-aged children have the opportunity to participate in a triathlon. Groups throughout the country train and race together. Many races also include a children's division or are held on a different day.

Noah Lam, Head Coach of the Lightning Warriors Triathlon Group on Long Island, said he works with children ages 7 to 17 in Western Nassau to Mount Sinai, Long Island. Every year, he organizes the Mini Maniac Youth Triathlon at Smith Point. Out of the group, he had one alumnus racing in the NCAA, one All-American, and one ranked #1 in 16-year-olds nationwide. "It makes me feel so good to coach these amazing kids."

Although kids can certainly compete, and they do compete, in this chapter, I'm focusing on high school triathletes because their preparation and performance can significantly influence their opportunities for college recruitment, scholarships, and participation in collegiate-level triathlon programs. Excelling at this stage can open doors to higher education and elite athletic circles, laying a foundation for academic and athletic success.

USAT has been pushing to get more high school students from swimming and running teams into triathlon.

I recently spoke with Tim Yount of USAT. He told me, "USA Triathlon has created a high school program that not only caters to kids with no experience in the sport but one that can engage them with self-improvement concepts that will support a lifetime mission of general fitness and health. Those in our programs will find clubs a great social outlet for building friendships. They promote meeting kids where they are athletically and create a support system. USA Triathlon is building programs that allow kids to race when they are ready, both indoors and outdoors."

Triathlons offer many benefits to high school students:

- Triathlon is a multidiscipline sport involving swimming, cycling, and running. This variety ensures a full-body workout, improving cardiovascular health, strength, flexibility, and endurance.
- Regular participation in triathlons can significantly reduce stress, anxiety, and symptoms of depression among high schoolers. The endorphins released from physical activity act as a natural mood lifter.
- Balancing training for three sports with academic responsibilities and social life teaches high schoolers how to manage their time effectively. These skills are invaluable and transferable to many other areas of life.
- Training for and completing a triathlon requires significant discipline and perseverance. These traits are developed over time and can benefit students' academic pursuits and future careers.
- Triathlons offer a clear framework for setting personal goals, whether finishing a race, beating a personal best, or qualifying for more competitive events. Achieving these goals boosts self-confidence and demonstrates the value of hard work.
- Being part of a triathlon community can provide a sense of belonging and camaraderie. High schoolers can make new friends, find mentors, and enjoy a supportive environment that encourages personal growth.
- Participation in sports like triathlons can enhance college applications. It demonstrates commitment, effective time management, and the ability to balance extracurricular activities with academic responsibilities.

- Engaging in regular training instills healthy lifestyle habits that can last a lifetime. High schoolers learn the importance of nutrition, adequate rest, and injury prevention early.
- Completing a triathlon provides a tangible sense of accomplishment, regardless of the position one finishes. This can be incredibly empowering for high schoolers, boosting their self-esteem and encouraging them to take on new challenges.

Training for a triathlon as a high school student involves distinct considerations compared to preparing as an adult. Young athletes are still growing, so their training regimens must account for this. Emphasis should be placed on developing technique and endurance to promote healthy physical development and reduce the risk of injury.

Coaches and trainers working with high school triathletes should prioritize:

- Ensuring young athletes master the fundamentals of swimming, cycling, and running techniques before ramping up mileage.
- Incorporating strength and flexibility work to support overall athletic development and prevent overuse injuries.
- Recognizing that young bodies need ample time to recover and adapt, especially during periods of growth.
- Providing advice on proper nutrition to fuel training and support healthy growth and development.

Transitioning from high school sports to triathlon means embracing new challenges and rewards. High schoolers can expect to develop a broader athletic skill set, gain a deeper understanding of their physical and mental capabilities, and become part of a supportive global community. The journey from novice to seasoned triathlete is filled with learning experiences that extend far beyond the racecourse, teaching valuable life lessons about perseverance, discipline, and the joy of pursuing one's passions.

For high school students looking to venture into the triathlon world, the journey promises the thrill of competition, the opportunity for personal growth, and the chance to be part of a unique and welcoming community. With the right approach to training and a healthy balance with life's other commitments, anyone can indeed "tri" and find success and fulfillment in this multifaceted sport.

Collegiate-Level Triathlete

The college club triathlon is exciting. It allows college students of all genders, abilities, and backgrounds to represent their school in competitive multisport.

By participating in triathlons, students learn how to handle schoolwork while training for the sport. This helps them become good at managing their time, staying resilient during tough times, and collaborating effectively with others. In addition, competing in college can help them get noticed for large worldwide races, and they may even go pro.

QUICK TIPS

- USAT has been at the forefront of helping young people develop their potential in high school.
- Competing on a college club team can be fun, but it can also help students manage time and create an atmosphere where they can meet lifelong friends.

Noah Lam
Triathlete, Stony Brook, NY

I kept getting injured from running and only really thought about triathlon once a friend signed up for an Ironman and inspired me. So, I signed up for the Mighty North Fork Triathlon, a sprint race. It was a 500-meter swim in the open water, a 7-mile bike ride, and a 3.5-mile run. I didn't know how to swim, but I could swim just enough not to drown.

I went to LA Fitness for the first time and couldn't swim 25 yards without stopping. My kids were taking swim lessons at Saf-T-Swim, so I figured I could, too. I needed to learn fast, so I signed up for lessons, swimming among swim diapers, babies, and toddlers.

Knowing Mighty North Fork was open water, I realized I had to take lessons or risk drowning. Meanwhile, I herniated my L3, L4, L5, and S1 from a twisting exercise. I wasn't sure if I could do Mighty North Fork, so my wife Irene prepared to take my spot. My doctor suggested back surgery, but it didn't feel right. My mom recommended an acupuncturist, and I felt much better after a few months. I told Irene to get her own entry, which she did, and we decided to race together.

Then, I had a seizure at work. It was an eye-opener, reminding me that life is short.

Before the race, Irene and I attended a talk about transitions at a library by Jose Lopez, a local triathlete and coach.

When I first bought a wetsuit, I couldn't figure out how to get into it. On race day, I brought everything Jose had advised. As I laid out my transition area, I wondered, "What did I get myself into?"

Everyone touched me in the water. I didn't realize people would be so close. When I got tired, I switched to the backstroke, but a friend pointed out I was going the wrong way. When I finished the swim, I thanked God.

I got on my 30-year-old Schwinn bike from high school graduation, which I had expensively tuned up instead of buying a new one. I saw Irene's bike still in transition and wasn't sure if she was still in the water.

After the bike ride, I transitioned to the run. Crossing the finish line, I thought, "I'm finished." I thanked God it was over. The experience was uncomfortable, but finishing made me feel like I could do anything. The triathlon was an eye-opener.

The following year, I signed up for Ironman Arizona.

CHAPTER 48

Pregnancy and Beyond. . .

"In conversation with a female runner during the run of a 70.3. Her: I don't know which was more painful, this or giving birth. Me: I'm happy I'll never experience the other, so I'll believe you whichever one you pick."
–Pathetic Triathlete Member

While pregnancy is a beautiful phase in a woman's life, it raises questions for active triathletes. Can they continue to compete? If so, until when? And how soon can they get back on track post-pregnancy?

Can You Still Compete?

The answer is yes, but with specific considerations. Ask your OB-GYN to clear you for training.

During the first trimester, most women can continue their usual training regimen as long as they feel comfortable and their healthcare provider has given the green light. However, physical changes may necessitate adaptations to the training routine as the pregnancy progresses.

It's important to listen to your body during this time. Pregnancy affects everyone differently, and what works for one person may not work for another. The key is to maintain a healthy balance between staying fit and ensuring the safety of both mother and baby.

When Should You Stop?

There isn't a one-size-fits-all answer to this question. The point at which a woman should stop competing or training heavily depends on her personal comfort, health conditions, and advice from her healthcare provider.

As a general guideline, high-intensity workouts and competitions are typically discouraged after the first trimester. During pregnancy, the body undergoes significant changes, including weight gain, shifts in the center of gravity, and increased joint laxity. These changes can affect balance and coordination, increasing the risk of injury.

Getting Back to Triathlon Post-Pregnancy

Resuming training post-pregnancy should be a gradual process. It's generally recommended to wait at least six weeks after a vaginal birth and eight weeks after a C-section before starting light exercise, but always consult with your healthcare provider first.

Remember, your body has undergone significant changes, so patience is key. Start with light activities, such as walking or swimming, and then gradually reintroduce cycling and running as your strength and endurance improve.

Advice for Women

- Listen to Your Body. This cannot be stressed enough. If you feel tired or uncomfortable, take it as a sign that you need to slow down or rest.
- Stay Hydrated. Pregnancy increases your fluid needs. Stay well-hydrated, especially during workouts.
- Maintain a Healthy Diet. A balanced diet is crucial for you and your baby's health. Include plenty of fruits, vegetables, whole grains, lean protein, and healthy fats.
- Consult a Professional. Regular check-ups with your healthcare provider are essential during this time. Discuss your training routine and any concerns you may have with them.
- Join a Support Group. Connecting with other pregnant athletes can provide motivation, support, and practical advice.

While pregnancy may necessitate some changes to your triathlon training and competing, it certainly doesn't mean the end of your athletic journey. With careful planning, professional guidance, and listening to your body, you can successfully navigate pregnancy and beyond as a triathlete.

QUICK TIP

- You don't have to stop training or racing if you are pregnant. However, be sure to consult with your OB-GYN about triathlon training and racing.

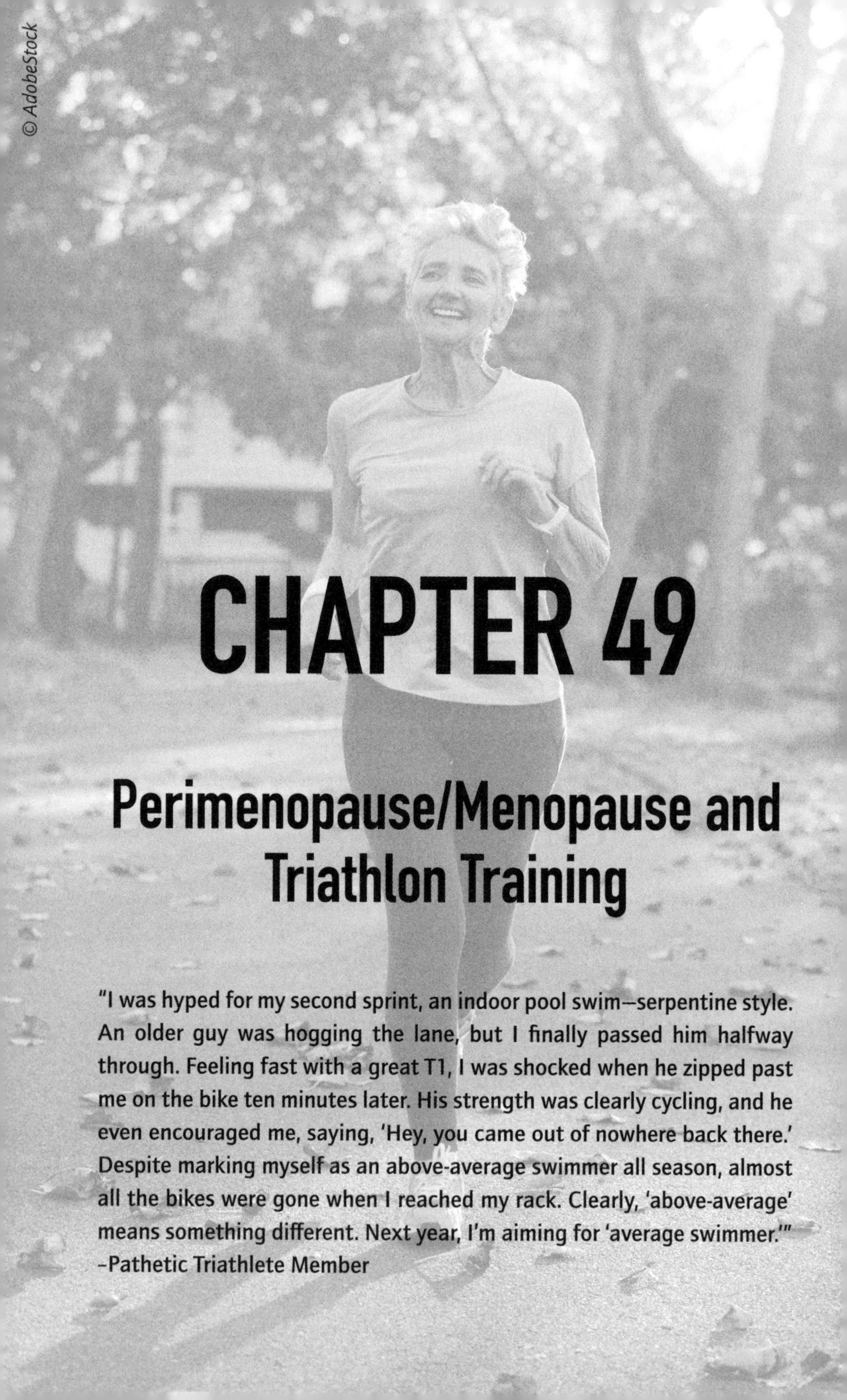

CHAPTER 49

Perimenopause/Menopause and Triathlon Training

"I was hyped for my second sprint, an indoor pool swim—serpentine style. An older guy was hogging the lane, but I finally passed him halfway through. Feeling fast with a great T1, I was shocked when he zipped past me on the bike ten minutes later. His strength was clearly cycling, and he even encouraged me, saying, 'Hey, you came out of nowhere back there.' Despite marking myself as an above-average swimmer all season, almost all the bikes were gone when I reached my rack. Clearly, 'above-average' means something different. Next year, I'm aiming for 'average swimmer.'"
–Pathetic Triathlete Member

Menopause, a natural biological process that marks the end of a woman's menstrual cycle, can bring with it specific challenges for female athletes. However, you can continue your triathlon training. Many women continue to train and compete successfully through menopause and beyond.

Menopause is characterized by a decrease in estrogen levels, which can lead to various symptoms like hot flashes, night sweats, and changes in energy levels. It is important to note that every woman's menopausal experience is unique. Some may perceive a minimal impact on their training, while others may need to make significant adjustments to their regimen.

After menopause, some symptoms, such as hot flashes and night sweats, may decrease, making exercise less of a barrier. However, changes in hormone levels can affect bone density and muscle mass, making strength training an essential part of your routine.

Training Strategies for Menopausal Athletes

Perimenopausal athletes can benefit from incorporating consistent rest days into their training schedule. They might need two to three rest days a week, allowing their bodies ample time to recover.

To manage hot flashes during workouts, consider cooling yourself before your session by draping a cold towel over your neck or drinking ice-cold fluid during your workout.

Heavy strength sessions followed by short interval bike workouts can be a practical approach. High-intensity plyometric workouts can also be beneficial.

Menopause may affect your metabolism, so focus on a balanced diet of protein, complex carbohydrates, and healthy fats to support your training and overall health.

While a balanced diet should provide most of the nutrients you need, some women find that certain supplements can help manage menopausal symptoms and support their training. Before starting any supplement regimen, please consult a healthcare professional to ensure it's safe.

Perimenopause and menopause are significant phases in a woman's life, but it doesn't have to slow down your triathlon goals. With the right strategies and adaptations, you can continue to train effectively and enjoy the sport you love.

QUICK TIPS

- Listen to your body and take extra rest days if you need them. Don't worry about the gains—with proper rest, you will achieve them!
- You may need to take supplements. Consult with your doctor or OB-GYN.

CHAPTER 50

Triathlon Training for Older Athletes

"One of the advantages of finishing 8 hours later for a half Ironman. Your wetsuit is all dry, and it's very easy to find your car in the parking lot."
–Pathetic Triathlete Member

Triathlon is a sport that transcends age boundaries. Age is not a barrier but a testament to one's enduring passion and commitment to fitness. You can skip this chapter if you are in your teens, 20s, 30s, or 40s. But it may also be relevant for people over 50.

As we age, physiological changes occur that can affect performance. These include decreased muscle mass, slower recovery times, reduced cardiovascular efficiency, and changes in flexibility. However, despite these changes, you can still train effectively and enjoy triathlon. You should adapt your training strategy to meet your body's needs.

Training Strategies for Older Athletes

Older athletes may require more time for recovery. Incorporate more rest days into your training schedule and consider incorporating active recovery activities, such as stretching or light swimming.

Regular strength training can help counteract muscle loss. Focus on compound movements, such as squats, lunges, and deadlifts, simultaneously working multiple muscle groups.

Incorporate flexibility and balance exercises into your routine to support joint health and lower the risk of injury.

While your pace may slow, cardiovascular exercise remains crucial. Maintain a regular cycling, running, and swimming routine, but listen to your body and adjust the intensity as needed.

Proper nutrition can aid in recovery. Focus on consuming a balanced diet rich in lean proteins, fruits, vegetables, and whole grains. Hydration is also essential, particularly during longer training sessions.

A positive mindset is valuable at any age but can be especially beneficial for older athletes. Embrace the journey, celebrate your progress, and remember that age is just a number. The goal is to enjoy the process of training and competing, regardless of pace or place in a race.

Being an older athlete is something to be celebrated. You demonstrate that passion, determination, and a love for sport have no age limit. While you might need to adapt your training approach, you can continue to reap the rewards of triathlon training. Listen to your body, consult with medical professionals as needed, and enjoy the journey!

QUICK TIPS

- You can still compete in triathlons if you are an older athlete. At a recent triathlon, an 85-year-old woman placed in her age group. I was so impressed!
- Practice mental preparation daily.

PART 7

NUTRITION

After you sign up for a race, find out what nutrition and hydration are on the course, then practice it on your own before the race. –Gwen Jorgensen

CHAPTER 51

Triathlon Nutrition

"For a while, I was dealing with some sugar-crash issues in daily life, so I was on a low glycemic diet. Even though sugar didn't seem to be an issue while exercising, I also tried staying low-carb during training. My first triathlon using low-carb fueling was a half-Ironman race. I was using for the first time a new 'aerodynamic' water bottle on my tri bike that narrowed at the bottom, and by the end of the ride, most of my low-carb powder had sunk to the bottom of the bottle and got stuck there. I was left with a bag of almonds to finish the 56-mile bike ride. I bonked with 40 minutes to go and used a gel, then had to use Gatorade when I got off the bike to run. After that experience, I went back to normal fueling for racing and I relearned the lesson of never using anything new on race day." –WeREndurance Member

Nutrition is a critical component of triathlon training and performance. What you eat can significantly impact your energy levels, recovery, strength, and overall endurance.

A well-rounded diet for a triathlete should include a balance of carbohydrates, proteins, and fats. Each plays a unique role in supporting your training and recovery.

Carbohydrates are the primary fuel for your muscles and brain during exercise. They should comprise 45-65% of your daily caloric intake. Eat complex carbs, which are long-lasting energy snacks, in whole grains, fruits, and vegetables. Unlike sugary snacks, which give you a quick energy boost and then crash, complex carbs take longer to break down, keeping you feeling full and energized for a longer time.

Proteins are crucial for muscle recovery and growth. They help repair the muscle tissue that gets broken down during training. Aim for lean proteins because they help repair and build your muscles without adding extra fat. Lean proteins, such as chicken, fish, tofu, and beans, give your body the essential building blocks to recover after all that swimming, biking, and running. This means you can get stronger and fitter without the added weight of extra fat slowing you down. These proteins keep you full longer, making you less likely to snack on junk food.

The International Society of Sports Nutrition recommends that endurance athletes consume 1.4–2.0 grams of protein per kg of body weight daily.

Healthy fats are a concentrated energy source and aid in the absorption of specific vitamins. Include foods rich in omega-3 fatty acids, such as avocados, nuts, seeds, and fatty fish like salmon.

How often you eat can depend on your training schedule and personal preferences. However, there are a few key times when nutrition is vital.

- Pre-Workout–A meal or snack high in carbohydrates before a workout can help ensure you have enough energy to perform at your best. Some people eat a banana or have a piece of toast.
- During Workout–Consuming carbs during workouts longer than an hour can help maintain energy levels. I get my carbs from INFINIT Nutrition, but sometimes I need an energy gel like GU.
- Post-Workout–a meal or snack combining protein and carbohydrates can aid recovery after a workout. Many say that you should have a protein shake here to build muscles.

Foods for Building Strength and Endurance

- Lean Proteins–Foods like lean meats, fish, eggs, and plant-based proteins provide the amino acids necessary for muscle repair and growth.
- Whole Grains–Foods such as brown rice, oatmeal, and whole grain bread provide sustained energy, helping to fuel longer workouts.
- Leafy Greens–Spinach, kale, and other leafy greens are packed with nutrients like iron, aiding oxygen transport during endurance activities.
- Beetroot–Some research suggests that beetroot can enhance athletic performance and endurance due to its high nitrate content.
- Bananas–Bananas are an excellent source of easily digestible carbohydrates and potassium, which helps maintain muscle function.

Nutrition serves as a powerful tool for improving triathlon training and performance. However, it's crucial to concentrate on macronutrients, which are the nutrients your body requires to remain healthy and energized. These include carbohydrates, proteins, and fats, all of which your body needs in significant amounts, unlike vitamins and minerals that are needed in smaller quantities.

By balancing macronutrients and timing your nutrition around your workouts, you can support your body's strength and endurance training needs.

QUICK TIPS

- Eat before you work out. Aim for healthy carbs, such as a banana or a piece of toast.
- Make sure you have different colors on your plate.

Sample Four-Day Menu for Sprint and Olympic Triathletes

Options for your weekdays: repeat any of these daily menu days/ choices Monday through Sunday.

Day 1

Breakfast

- 1 cup 2-4% milkfat plain Greek yogurt
- ⅓ cup granola (store-bought of choice, no more than 5 grams of fat per ⅓ cup serving)
- ½ cup blueberries
- 1 peach, nectarine, or 1 cup melon
- *25-30 grams protein*

Snack

- 1 ounce cheddar or mozzarella cheese
- 10 whole grain crackers (example: Wheat Thins or six Triscuits)
- 1 cup grapes or cherries
- *10 grams protein*

Lunch

- One can of tuna or four ounces of chicken mixed with two tablespoons of mayonnaise or three tablespoons of plain Greek yogurt wrapped in an eight-inch whole wheat tortilla.
- 1 small red bell pepper, sliced
- 1 ounce pretzels, no surface salt
- *24 grams protein*

Snack

- 1 cup melon (cantaloupe or watermelon)
- 5 walnuts or 10 almonds

- 1 hard-boiled egg or one string cheese
- *14 grams protein*

Dinner
- 5 ounces chicken breast, or skinless thigh, coated in one tablespoon pesto, or one tablespoon mustard mixed with one tablespoon honey, baked
- 1 cup whole wheat pasta mixed with one tablespoon pesto or ⅓ cup marinara sauce
- 10 asparagus spears or 1 cup broccoli mixed with one tablespoon olive oil, salt, and pepper, grilled or roasted
- *31 grams protein*

Snack
- 1 cup fresh fruit of choice and one large rice cake of choice

Day 2
Breakfast
- One slice 100% whole wheat bread
- ½ avocado
- Sliced tomato
- 2 eggs, scrambled or fried in a drizzle of olive oil
- 1 apple or ½ cup unsweetened apple sauce
- *18 grams protein*

Snack
- 1 cup grapes or cherries
- 5 walnuts or 10 almonds
- *9 grams protein*

Dinner

- Black bean and corn quesadilla with ½ cup black beans, ⅓ cup corn kernels, and ¼ cup shredded cheddar or mozzarella cheese on an 8-inch whole wheat tortilla
- ¼ cup salsa and ¼ cup guacamole or ¼ avocado sliced
- Garden salad of dark greens, cucumbers, carrots, and a drizzle of olive oil
- *24 grams protein*

Snack

- Protein shake: 2 scoops vanilla whey protein powder mixed with 1 cup unsweetened vanilla almond milk
- *29 grams protein*

Dinner

- 6 ounces turkey burger on a 100% whole wheat bun with lettuce, tomato
- 1 zucchini sliced into spears, or one cup broccoli roasted with 1 tablespoon olive oil
- 1 medium white or sweet potato, sliced into French fries and baked with 1 tablespoon olive oil, or baked whole
- *39 grams protein*

Snack

- 2 tablespoons peanut butter
- 1 medium banana
- *13 grams protein*

Day 3
Breakfast

- 1 cup cooked oatmeal in milk of choice

- 2 tablespoons peanut or almond butter, the only ingredients are nuts, perhaps salt
- ½ cup blueberries
- *12 grams protein*

Snack

- 1 peach, or nectarine, or 1 cup melon
- 5 walnuts or 10 almonds
- Protein shake: 1 scoop vanilla whey protein powder mixed with 1 cup unsweetened vanilla almond milk or milk of choice
- *37 grams protein*

Lunch

- Tuna melt with 4 ounces of canned tuna mixed with ¼ avocado, 1 ounce of cheddar or mozzarella cheese, and sliced tomato on two slices of 100% whole wheat bread
- Garden salad of greens, cucumbers, and carrots with a drizzle of olive oil and lemon or vinegar
- *34 grams protein*

Snack

- 1 cup raw carrots and unlimited cucumber
- 4 tablespoons hummus or 4 tablespoons guacamole
- *8 grams protein*

Dinner

- 5 ounces shredded chicken or 4 ounces cooked shrimp or fish, or tofu, 1 ounce shredded cheddar or mozzarella cheese, quesadilla in an 8-inch whole wheat tortilla with ¼ cup black beans and shredded greens
- ¼ cup salsa

- 1 cup cooked veggies of choice, such as zucchini, asparagus, broccoli, or green beans with lemon
- *46 grams protein*

Snack

- 1 apple
- 2 tablespoons almond or peanut butter
- *8 grams protein*

Day 4

(Make this the days before your biggest training mornings (typically Friday and Saturday))

Breakfast

- 2 slices simple carb bread, such as potato bread or roll, English muffin, small plain bagel, or two regular waffles
- 1 ½ tablespoons peanut butter with a drizzle of honey or 1 tablespoon of fruit jam
- 1 banana
- *14 grams protein*

Snack

- 1 cup 2–4% milkfat plain Greek yogurt
- ½ cup raspberries or blueberries or ¾ cup strawberries or watermelon
- *24 grams protein*

Lunch

- Salad with 3 ounces leftover protein of choice, ½ cup chickpeas, ¼ cup olives, ¼ cup feta cheese, tomatoes, cucumbers, and a drizzle of olive oil and balsamic vinegar

- One 6-inch 100% whole wheat pita bread or wrap
- *21 grams protein*

Snack

- 1 cup raw carrots or cucumbers
- ¼ cup guacamole or hummus
- 1 hard-boiled egg
- *10 grams protein*

Dinner

- 5–6 ounces grilled salmon or chicken or 4 ounces tofu or lean ground beef or turkey
- 1 medium baked sweet potato or ¾ cup white or Jasmine rice
- ¾ cup frozen peas and carrots
- *32 grams protein*

Snack

- 2 squares of 70% dark chocolate
- 5 walnuts or 10 almonds

This information was provided by Staci Blanket, a triathlete, running coach, certified fitness professional, and the owner of Positive Plates Nutrition, Sports and Wellness Nutrition Planning, Coaching, and Consulting Services in Bethpage, NY.

CHAPTER 52

Supplements, Gels, and Hydration for Triathletes

"I did my first Ironman AZ during radiation in 2013, and I was worried about nutrition, so I put a foot-long subway sandwich in my shorts on the bike. It was a little salty, but it was the best sandwich I've ever had, true story! LOL I have a video somewhere of this." –Pathetic Triathlete Member

Supplements can be an effective way to fill nutritional gaps and support your training. However, they should not replace a balanced diet; rather, they should complement it.

Protein powder is vital for muscle repair and recovery after intense training sessions. Whey protein is popular due to its rapid absorption rate. Plant-based proteins like pea or hemp are excellent alternatives for those with dietary restrictions.

Omega-3 fatty acids, found in fish oil supplements, are essential fats with anti-inflammatory properties that aid recovery. They also support heart health, a crucial consideration for endurance athletes.

Iron is vital for producing hemoglobin, which carries oxygen to your muscles. Iron deficiency can lead to fatigue and reduced performance.

Vitamin D supports bone health and immune function. Many people are deficient in vitamin D, particularly those residing in northern climates or who primarily train indoors.

Magnesium aids muscle function, nerve transmission, and energy production. It's also vital for maintaining electrolyte balance. I take magnesium to help alleviate my cramps when I work out.

Energy gels are concentrated sources of quick-absorbing carbohydrates. They provide immediate energy boosts during prolonged exercise. They're small, lightweight, and easy to consume on the go. I always bring a GU gel for long runs or rides. Some people like the GU Chews. Either one is good.

Hydration is not just about water; it's also about replenishing electrolytes lost through sweat. An effective hydration strategy includes regularly drinking small amounts of fluid throughout the event. Many hydration additives are available, including INFINIT Nutrition, Skratch, Nuun, and GU Tablets.

Always consult with a healthcare provider before starting any supplement regimen.

QUICK TIPS

- Everyone's body responds differently to supplements and nutrition strategies. Experimenting during training is essential to find what works best for you before the event.
- If you are training for more than 30 minutes, don't just drink water. As noted above, add electrolytes and a supplement to your water.

Supplements

Supplements have been a topic for discussion for years in the health and fitness community. While some argue that a balanced diet should provide all the necessary nutrients, others suggest that supplements can help fill nutritional gaps or enhance performance. Craig Dinkel, founder of BioTropic Labs, firmly believes in the latter.

He competed on a world-class level in sprint freestyle and fly swimming and was coached by two Olympic coaches. In a recent conversation, he shared his insights on why taking supplements is essential.

Craig told me that while training for the Olympic team, he worked with Dr. Ed Wagner, a highly skilled nutritionist and chiropractor. Dr. Wagner designed a comprehensive nutritional program for Craig, including a custom blend of minerals and vitamins.

Craig described exceptional results. He believes the right combination of diet and supplementation can significantly improve performance.

When asked about his recommendations for a beginning triathlete, Craig advised focusing on blood oxygen delivery and recovery-oriented supplements. He also stressed the importance of finding the correct dosage that yields the desired performance results without overloading the digestive system.

EPILOGUE: THE TRIATHLETE WITHIN

As we conclude this journey, remember that unlocking the triathlon is possible and that anyone can participate in a triathlon. You've taken the first brave steps into a world that tests your endurance, resilience, and spirit. You've chosen to challenge yourself physically, mentally, and emotionally. And for that, you should be immensely proud.

Triathlon is more than a sport; it's a testament to human will and determination. It's about pushing past your limits, overcoming obstacles, and realizing that you can do more than you ever imagined.

Whether standing at the starting line of your first race or crossing the finish line after many, remember this: every step you take, every stroke you swim, every pedal you push, you're not just moving forward in the race; you're moving forward in life.

Triathlons teach us valuable lessons about perseverance, strength, and the power of belief. They show us that setbacks are stepping stones to comebacks and that our most challenging moments often lead to our most significant victories.

So, keep training, keep pushing, and keep believing in yourself. It's not about how fast you go but how far you've come. It's about the journey, the growth, and the person you become along the way.

Ultimately, it doesn't matter if you finish first or last. What matters is that you dared to start, the determination to keep going, and the resilience to finish. That's what makes you a triathlete.

Unlocking the Triathlon: A Beginner's Guide to Triathlon Training is your gateway to discovering the athlete within you. The path ahead may challenge you, but every effort, every step, and every stroke takes you closer to becoming the best version of yourself.

You've taken the first step by believing in your ability to "tri" and now, the finish line is yours to define. Celebrate this beginning, trust the process, and get ready to unlock your true potential.

APPENDIX A: TRIATHLON CHECKLIST

Here's a comprehensive checklist to ensure you have everything you need for race day, divided by segments: swim, bike, run, and transition. Pack your gear the night before the race to avoid any last-minute stress.

Check out www.*ATriathletesDiary.com/Discounts* for the latest discounts on all things swim, bike, and run.

Pre-Race Essentials

- Race confirmation and ID (for packet pickup)
- Triathlon race kit
- Timing chip and strap (provided by the race)
- Race bib and safety pins (also provided by the race)
- Race belt
- Body marking pen (if not provided by the race)
- Sunscreen (water-resistant)
- Nutrition (energy bars, gels, etc.)
- Hydration (water bottles, electrolyte drinks)
- Transition bag

Swim

- Goggles (consider bringing an extra pair)
- Swim cap (usually provided by the race, but bring your own just in case)
- Wetsuit (if the water temperature is within the legal range for wetsuit use)
- Anti-chafe balm (for neck and other areas prone to chafing from the wetsuit)
- Earplugs and/or nose plugs (if needed)
- A small towel

Bike

- Bicycle (ensure it is tuned, charged, and race-ready)
- Helmet (check for no cracks and that it fits well)
- Cycling shoes and socks (if wearing)
- Bike computer (if you use one)
- Sunglasses or clear eye protection
- Water bottles (filled with water or sports drink)
- Bike repair kit (spare tube, tire levers, CO_2 cartridges or mini pump, multi-tool)
- Race number belt or bike frame number (as required by the race and given out prior to the race)

Run

- Running shoes (with quick-lace system if preferred)
- Hat or visor
- Additional nutrition or hydration (if carrying on the run)
- Race number (provided by the race)
- Run belt (optional)

Transition

- Transition mat or towel (to set up your gear)
- Large water bottle (for rinsing feet after the swim or drinking)
- Plastic bag (for wet gear post-race)
- First aid kit (band-aids, antiseptic wipes, blister patches)
- Portable pump (for last-minute bike tire pressure adjustments)

Miscellaneous

- Watch or GPS device (fully charged)
- Post-race recovery snacks or drinks

- Camera or smartphone (for capturing those memorable moments)
- Money and ID (in a waterproof pouch, just in case)
- Spectator essentials (chairs, signs, etc., if you have friends/family coming)
- Post-race change of clothes and shoes

Night Before Checklist

- Check the weather forecast and adjust your gear as needed
- Review racecourse maps and schedule
- Plan your morning timeline (wake-up time, breakfast, arrival at the venue)
- Visualize your race and transitions
- Get a good night's sleep

This checklist should help you arrive at your triathlon feeling prepared and confident. The key to a successful race day is having all your gear and approaching the event with a positive mindset and readiness to adapt to any situation. Good luck and enjoy the race!

APPENDIX B: TRAINING PLANS

20-Week Sprint Program for a New Triathlete

This program is designed for individuals who are new to swimming, biking, and running, but have prior experience with swimming.

If the swim is not specified, it's a freestyle swim. Everything is in meters (m), so if you are at a "yard" pool, do the same workout. Codes are as follows:

- WU: means warm-up
- DS: means drill set
- MS: means main set
- CD: cool-down
- Strength: strength training
- Swim: this means freestyle swim

Take a break when you need it. Try to stick with a 30-second rest. Also, I included two strength workouts. They should be approximately 30 minutes.

Finally, you can move the schedule around. If you have something on a particular day, change it. This program is a guideline for you to follow but it can be changed.

Weeks 1–4: Building the Foundation

	Week 1	Week 2	Week 3	Recover Week 4
Monday	**Swim** 200 m **WU:** 25 m **Kick** 25 m with fins and paddles **Pull:** 50 m with a pull buoy and paddles **Kick:** 50 m **Swim:** 50 m	**Swim** 250 m **WU:** 50 m **Kick** 25 m with fins and paddles **Pull:** 50 m with a pull buoy and paddles **Kick:** 25m **Swim:** 25 m Pull buoy and **paddles:** 50 m CD: 25 m	**Swim** 300 m (rest as needed) **WU:** 75 m **Kick:** 25 m with fins and paddles **Pull:** 50 m with a pull buoy and paddles **Kick:** 25 m **Swim:** 50 m **CD:** pull buoy and paddles 50 m, 25 m easy	**Swim** 200 m **WU:** 25 m **Kick:** 25 m with fins and paddles **Pull:** 50 m with a pull buoy and paddles **Kick:** 50 m **Swim:** 25 m **CD:** Pull buoy and paddles 25 m
Tuesday	**Run** 30 min easy pace, **strength**	**Bike** 35 min easy pace, **strength**	**Bike** 40 min easy pace, **strength**	**Bike** 30 min **easy** pace
Wednesday	Rest day	Rest day	Rest day	Rest day
Thursday	**Run** 0.5 miles	**Run** 1 mile	**Run** 1.5 miles followed by strength	**Run** 1 mile
Friday	**Swim** 200 m **WU:** 50 m **DS:** 2 drills from book, 25 drill/ 25 swim **CD:** 50 m swim	**Swim** 250 m (rest as needed) **WU:** 50 m **Kick:** 25 m with fins and paddles **Pull:** 50 m with a pull buoy and paddles **Kick:** 25 m **Swim:** 50 m **CD:** 50 m pull buoy and paddles	**Swim** 300 m (rest as needed) **WU:** 50 m **Kick:** 25 m with fins and paddles **Pull:** 75 m with a pull buoy and paddles **Kick:** 25 m **Swim:** 50 m **Kick:** 25 m **CD:** Pull buoy and paddles 50 m	**Swim** 200 m (rest as needed) **WU:** 50 m **DS:** 2 drills from book, 25 drill/ 25 swim **CD:** 50 m swim
Saturday	**Bike** 30 min	**Bike** 35 min easy pace, **strength**	**Bike** 40 min easy pace	**Bike** 30 min easy pace
Sunday	Rest day	Rest day	**Run** 1.5 miles	Rest day

Weeks 5-8: Increasing Endurance

	Week 5	Week 6	Week 7	Week 8 (Recovery)
Monday	**Swim** 400 m **WU:** 100 m straight, nice and easy **DS:** 100 m in drills (see section on drills) **MS:** 50 m, rest for 20 seconds; 50 m free, rest 20 seconds; 50 m free, rest 20 seconds **CD:** 2 × 25 m easy	**Swim** 450 m (rest as needed) **WU:** 50 m **DS:** pick 4 out of the group and focus on them for 25 m. Do drill for 25/then swim for 25 **MS:** 100 m straight with or without fins; 50 m paddles and buoy **CD:** 50 m easy	**Swim** 500 m (rest as needed) **WU:** 100 m no stopping **DS:** Pick 2, do drill for 25/swim back 25 **MS:** Swim 50 m; swim 150 m; swim 50 m **CD:** 50 m	**Swim** 400 m **WU:** 100 m straight, nice and easy **DS:** 100 m in drills (see section on drills) **MS:** 50 m, rest for 20 seconds; 50 m free, rest 20 seconds; 50 m free, rest 20 seconds **CD:** 2 × 25 m easy
Tuesday	**Bike** 50 minutes easy pace, **Strength**	**Bike** 55 min easy bike pace, **Strength**	**Bike** 1 hour easy pace, **Strength**	**Bike** 50 minutes easy pace
Wednesday	Rest day	Rest day	Rest day	Rest day
Thursday	**Run** 1.5 miles	**Run** 1.5 miles, **Strength**	**Run** 2 miles, **Strength**	**Run** 1.5 miles
Friday	**Swim** 400 m (rest as needed) **Swim** 400 m any way you want with any stroke but keep moving forward.	**Swim** 450 m (rest as needed) **WU:** 50 m **MS:** 200 m free no stopping; 50 m; 100 m **CD:** 50 m backstroke	**Swim** 500 m (rest as needed) **WU:** 100 m of drills your choice **MS:** 100 m swim; 100 m with fins and paddles; 100 m with pull buoy and paddles **CD:** 100 m swim easy	**Swim** 400 m (rest as needed) **Swim** 400 m any way you want with any stroke but keep moving forward.
Saturday	**Bike** 50 minutes easy pace, **Strength**	**Bike** 55 min easy bike pace	**Bike** 1 hour easy pace	**Bike** 50 minutes easy pace
Sunday	**Run** 1.5 miles	**Run** 1.5 miles	**Run** 2 miles	**Rest** day

Weeks 9–12: Building Strength and Speed

	Week 9	Week 10	Week 11	Week 12 (Recovery)
Monday	**Swim** 600 m (rest as needed) **WU:** 200 m straight, nice and easy, any stroke **DS:** 100 m in drills (see section on drills) **MS:** 100 m, rest for 20 seconds; 50 free, rest 20 seconds; 100 m free, rest 20 seconds **CD:** 50 m easy	**Swim** 650 m (rest as needed) **WU:** 100 m **DS:** 6 × 25 drill/25 swim your choice from the list in the book **MS:** 100 m Fast; 50 m Fast, 150 m easy **CD:** 50 m easy, any stroke Strength	**Swim** 700 m (rest as needed) **WU:** 150 m **MS:** 150 m with fins; 100 m with fins and paddles; 75 m with pull buoy and paddles; 50 m with kickboard and fins; 25 m swim **CD:** 150 m mixed strokes Strength	**Swim** 600 m (rest as needed) **WU:** 200 m straight, nice and easy, any stroke **DS:** 100 m in drills (see section on drills) **MS:** 100 m, rest for 20 seconds; 50 m free, rest 20 seconds; 100 m free, rest 20 seconds **CD:** 50 m easy
Tuesday	**Bike** 1 hour 15 minutes incorporate interval training. See chapter 26. **Strength**	**Bike** 1 hour 20 minutes incorporate interval training. See chapter 26.	**Bike** 1 hour 25 minutes incorporate interval training. See chapter 26. **Strength**	**Bike** 1 hour 15 minutes moderate pace. **Strength**
Wednesday	Rest day	Rest day	Rest day	Rest day
Thursday	**Run** 2.5 miles, **Strength**	**Run** 2.5 miles, **Strength**	**Run** 2 miles, **Strength**	**Run** 2 miles
Friday	**Swim** 600 m (rest as needed) **WU:** 150 m **MS:** 50 m Fast; 50 m easy; 50 m Fast; 50 m easy; 50 m Fast **CD:** 200 m easy, any stroke	**Swim** 650 m (rest as needed) **WU:** 100 m Swim **DS:** 6 × 25 Drill/25 Swim your choice from the drills section **MS:** 100 m Fast; 50 m Fast, 150 m easy **CD:** 50 m easy	**Swim** 700 m (rest as needed) **WU:** 150 m **MS:** 150 m with fins; 100 m with fins and paddles; 75 m with pull buoy and paddles; 50 m with kickboard and fins; 25 m swim **CD:** 150 m mixed strokes	**Swim** 600 m (rest as needed) **WU:** 150 m **MS:** 50 m Fast; 50 m easy; 50 m Fast; 50 m easy; 50 m Fast **CD:** 200 m easy, any stroke
Saturday	**Bike** 1 hour 15 minutes moderate pace	**Bike** 1 hour 20 minutes moderate pace, **Strength**	**Bike** 1 hour 25 minutes moderate pace	**Bike** 1 hour 15 minutes moderate pace
Sunday	Run 2.5 miles	**Run** 2.5 miles	**Run** 3 miles	**Run** 2 miles

Weeks 13-16: Increasing Intensity

	Week 13	Week 14	Week 15	Week 16 (Recovery)
Monday	**Swim** 800 m (rest as needed) open-water swim strength	**Swim** 850 m (rest as needed) **WU:** 250 m **DS:** 6 × 25 drill/25 swim your choice from the list in the book **MS:** 100 m FAST; 50 m Slow; 50 m FAST **CD:** 100 m Easy	**Swim** 900 m (rest as needed) open-water swimming Strength	**Swim** 800 m (rest as needed) **WU:** 100 m **MS:** 300 m moderate; 200 m moderate; 100 m moderate **CD:** 100 m Easy
Tuesday	**Bike** 1 hour 35 minutes incorporate interval training. See chapter 26. **Strength**	**Bike** 1 hour 40 minutes moderate pace, followed by **Strength**	**Bike** 1 hour 45 minutes moderate pace	**Bike** 1 hour 35 minutes moderate pace
Wednesday	Rest day	Rest day	Rest day	Rest day
Thursday	**Run** 3 miles with intervals, **Strength**	**Run** 3 miles, intervals or Fartlek (see chapter 30 for more details), **Strength**	**Run** 3.5 miles, intervals, **Strength**	**Run** 2 miles
Friday	**Swim** 800 m (rest as needed) **WU:** 150 m swim **MS:** 100 m Fast; 50 m Slow; 100 m Fast; 50 m Slow; 100 m Fast; 100 m Slow; 100 m easy **CD:** 50 m slow	**Swim** 850 m (rest as needed) open-water swim	**Swim** 900 m (rest as needed) **WU:** 100 m Easy MS: 200 m × 3 moderate; 50 m × 2 Fast, 15-second rest **CD:** 100 m Swim	**Swim** 800 m (rest as needed) **WU:** 150 m swim **MS:** 100 m Fast; 50 m Slow; 100 m Fast; 50 m slow; 100 m Fast; 50 m slow; 100 m easy **CD:** 100 m slow
Saturday	**Brick** **Bike** 1 hour 35 minutes moderate pace, followed by a short 15-minute **run**.	**Brick** **Bike** 1 hour 40 minutes moderate pace, **run** off bike 15 minutes	**Brick** **Bike** 1 hour 45 minutes moderate pace, with a 20-minute **run** off the bike	**Bike** 1 hour 35 minutes moderate pace
Sunday	Rest day	Rest day	**Run** 2 miles easy	**Walk**

Weeks 17–20: Peak Training and Tapering

	Week 17	Week 18	Week 19 (Taper week)	Week 20 (Race week)
Monday	**Swim** 1,000 m (rest as needed) **WU:** 200 m easy **DS:** 4 × 25 drill of choice/25 swim **MS:** 200 m swim easy; 100 m breaststroke; 100 m Swim Fast **CD:** 200 m easy	**Swim** 1,100 m (rest as needed) **WU:** 200 m swim **MS:** 300 m swim; 200 paddles/pull buoy; 100 m kick with board and paddles;100 m swim **CD:** 200 m swim	**Swim** 800 m (rest as needed) **WU:** 100 m **MS:** 300 m moderate pace; 200 m moderate pace; 100 m moderate pace **CD:** 100 m easy	**Swim** 500 m (rest as needed) 2 sets of 250 m
Tuesday	**Bike** 2 hours moderate pace, **Strength**	**Bike** 2 hours 10 minutes moderate pace, **Strength**	**Bike** 1 hour 30 minutes easy pace	**Bike** 1 hour easy pace
Wednesday	Rest day	Rest day	Rest day	Rest day
Thursday	**Run** 2.0 miles, **Strength**	**Run** 4 miles, with intervals, **Strength**	**Run** 4 miles	**Run** 2 miles easy
Friday	**Swim** 1,000 m (rest as needed) Open-water training with intervals	**Swim** 1,200 m (rest as needed) open-water swimming	**Swim** 800 m (rest as needed) **WU:** 150 m swim **MS:** 100 m Fast; 50 m slow; 100 m Fast; 50 m slow; 100 m Fast; 50 m slow; 100 m easy **CD:** 100 m slow	**Swim** 500 m (rest as needed) **WU:** 100 m **MS:** 200 m Fast; 50 m slow; 50 m moderate **CD:** 100 m
Saturday	**Bike** 2 hours moderate pace, run off the bike for 20 minutes	**Brick** **Bike** 2 hours 10 minutes moderate pace, 15-minute **run** off bike	**Bike** 1 hour 30 minutes easy pace	Rest day
Sunday	**Run** 4 miles easy pace	**Run** 2 miles easy	Rest day	Race day!

20-week Sprint Program for an Experienced Triathlete

The following is a 20-week training plan for an experienced triathlete aiming to podium in their next sprint triathlon. This plan includes endurance, speed, strength training, and recovery periods to ensure peak performance on race day. The plan also incorporates brick workouts (back-to-back bike and run) to prepare for the transitions. In addition, when the swim portion says swim, that means freestyle swim. If it doesn't specify, it is always freestyle. Refer to the book on the bike and the run sections for more information.

If the swim is not specified, it's a freestyle swim. Everything is in meters (m), so if you are at a "yard" pool, do the same workout. Codes are as follows:

- WU: means warm-up
- DS: means drill set
- MS: means main set
- CD: cool-down
- Strength: strength training
- Swim: this means freestyle swim

Take a break when you need it. Try to stick with a 30-second rest. Also, I included two strength workouts. They should be approximately 30 minutes.

Finally, you can move the schedule around. If you have something on a particular day, change it. This program is a guideline for you to follow but it can be changed.

Weeks 1–4: Base Building Phase

	Week 1	Week 2	Week 3	Week 4 (Recovery)
Monday	**Swim** 1,500 m (technique focus) **WU:** 200 m **DS:** Choose 4 × 25 drill/25 swim **MS:** 400 m swim with fins and paddles; 300 m swim with fins; 200 m swim with pull buoy and paddles; 100 m swim **CD:** 100 m easy, any stroke	**Swim** 1,600 m (technique focus) **WU:** 300 m **DS:** 100 m kick with kickboard and fins; 2 Drills at 25 drill/25 swim **MS:** 100 m × 6; 50 m × 4 – Fast with 30 second rest **CD:** 300 m	**Swim** 1,700 m (technique focus) **WU:** 14 drills from book, do each for 50 m, rest 15 seconds **MS:** 300 m swim slow; 300 m swim moderate; 300 m swim Fast **CD:** 100 free easy	**Swim** 1,500 m (technique focus) **WU:** 200 m DS: Choose 2 × 25 drill/25 swim **MS:** 400 m swim with fins and paddles; 300 m swim with fins; 200 m swim with pull buoy and paddles;100 m swim **CD:** 200 m easy, any stroke
Tuesday	**Bike** 40 minutes easy + **Strength**	**Bike** 45 minutes easy + Strength	**Bike** 50 minutes easy + Strength	**Bike** 40 minutes easy + Strength
Wednesday	**Run** 5K tempo run	**Run** 6K tempo run	**Run** 7K tempo run	**Run** 5K tempo run
Thursday	**Swim** 1,500 m (endurance) **WU:** 200 m **DS:** 4 × 25 drill/25 swim **MS:** 400 m swim with fins; 300 m swim with paddles and fins; 200 m swim with pull buoy; 100 m swim **CD:** 100 m easy **Strength**	**Swim** 1,600 m (endurance) **WU:** 400 m **MS:** 6 × 100 m, 30 second rest; 4 × 50 m Fast, 10 second rest **CD:** 400, broken up with back, breast, and free **Strength**	**Swim** 1,700 m (endurance) **WU:** 400 m easy **MS:** 400 m with fins and paddles; 300 m fins only; 200 m paddles only; 100 m swim Fast **CD:** 300 m easy, any stroke **Strength**	**Swim** 1,800 m (endurance) **WU:** 300 m DS: 4 × 25 drill/25 swim **MS:** 400 m swim with fins; 300 m swim with paddles and fins; 200 m swim with pull buoy; 100 m swim **CD:** 300 m easy **Strength**
Friday	Rest or Active Recovery (like walking, yoga, etc.)	Rest or active recovery	Rest or Active Recovery	Rest or Active Recovery
Saturday	**Bike** 60 minutes	**Bike** 70 minutes	**Bike** 80 minutes	**Bike** 60 minutes
Sunday	**Brick** **Bike** 40 minutes + **Run** 1 mile	**Brick** **Bike** 45 minutes + **Run** 1 mile	**Brick** **Bike** 50 minutes + **Run** 1.5 miles	**Brick** **Bike** 40 minutes + **Run** 1 mile

Weeks 5–8: Build Phase

	Week 5	Week 6	Week 7	Week 8
Monday	**Swim** 2,000 m (intervals) **WU:** 300 m straight, nice and easy **MS:** 400 m swim; 300 m swim; 200 m pull/paddles; 300 m swim; 200 m fins/paddles **CD:** 300 m easy	**Swim** 2,100 m (intervals) open-water swim	**Swim** 2,200 m (intervals) **WU:** 400 m **DS:** Pick 4, drill for 25/swim 25 **Kick:** 200 m with board and fins **MS:** 400 m swim; Fast 50s × 10; 300 m easy swim **CD:** 200 m easy	**Swim** 2,300 m (intervals) open-water swim
Tuesday	**Bike** 60 minutes moderate + **Strength**	**Bike** 65 minutes moderate + **Strength**	**Bike** 70 minutes moderate + **Strength**	**Bike** 75 minutes moderate + **Strength**
Wednesday	**Run** 5K interval run	**Run** 6K interval run	**Run** 6K interval run	**Run** 7K interval run
Thursday	**Swim** 2,000 m (endurance) open-water swim **Strength**	**Swim** 2,100 m (endurance) open-water swim **Strength**	**Swim** 2,200 m (endurance) open-water swim **Strength**	**Swim** 2,300 m (endurance) open-water swim **Strength**
Friday	Rest or Active Recovery	Rest or Active Recovery	Rest or Active Recovery	Rest or Active Recovery
Saturday	**Bike** 100 minutes	**Bike** 110 minute	**Bike** 120 minutes	**Bike** 130 minutes
Sunday	**Brick:** **Bike** 60 minutes + **Run** 1.5 miles	**Brick:** **Bike** 65 minutes + **Run** 2 miles	**Brick:** **Bike** 70 minutes + **Run** 2 miles	**Brick:** **Bike** 75 minutes + **Run** 2.5 miles

Weeks 9–13: Peak Volume Phase

	Week 9 (Recovery)	Week 10	Week 11	Week 12	Week 13 (Recovery)
Monday	**Swim** 2,000 m (intervals) **WU:** 300 m straight, nice and easy **MS:** 400 m; 300 m swim; 200 m pull/ paddles; 300 m with fins; 200 m with fins and paddles **CD:** 300 m swim easy	**Swim** 2,500 m (speed work) open-water swim	**Swim** 2,600 m (speed work) open-water swim	**Swim** 2,700 m (speed work) open-water swim	**Swim** 2,500 m (speed work) open-water swim
Tuesday	**Bike** 60 minutes moderate + **Strength**	**Bike** 85 minutes moderate + **Strength**	**Bike** 90 minutes moderate + **Strength**	**Bike** 95 minutes moderate + **Strength**	**Bike** 85 minutes moderate + **Strength**
Wednesday	**Run** 5K interval run	**Run** 8K interval run	**Run** 9K interval run	**Run** 10K interval run	**Run** 4K interval run
Thursday	**Swim** 2,000 m (endurance) open-water swim	**Swim** 2,500 m (endurance) open-water swim **Strength**	**Swim** 2,600 m (endurance) open-water swim **Strength**	**Swim** 2,700 m (endurance) **WU:** 500 m **DS:** 4 × 50 m, choice **MS:** 100 m × 10 Fast, 30-second rest; 500 m endurance **CD:** 2 × 250 m easy **Strength**	**Swim** 2,500 m (endurance) open-water swim **Strength**
Friday	Rest or Active Recovery	Rest or Active Recovery	Rest or Active Recovery	Rest or Active Recovery	Rest or Active Recovery
Saturday	**Bike** 100 minutes	**Bike** 150 minutes	**Bike** 160 minutes	**Bike** 170 minutes	**Bike** 150 minutes
Sunday	**Brick**: **Bike** 60 minutes + **Run** 1 mile	**Brick Bike** 85 minutes + **Run** 1.5 miles	**Bric:** **Bike** 90 minutes + **Run** 2 miles	**Brick:** **Bike** 95 minutes + **Run** 2 miles	**Brick Bike** 85 minutes + **Run** 1 mile

Weeks 14–17: Speed and Intensity Phase

	Week 14	Week 15	Week 16	Week 17 (Recovery)
Monday	**Swim** 2,900 m (intervals); see chapter 20 **Run:** 5 miles easy	**Swim** 3,000 m (intervals) **WU:** 500 m free **DS:** 6 × 100 m your choice of drills **MS:** 500 m fins and paddles; 400 m fins only; 300 m paddles and pull buoy only; 200 m swim easy; 100 m kick with fins **CD:** 400 m easy **Run:** 5 miles easy	**Swim** 3,100 m (intervals) open-water swim **Strength**	**Swim** 2,900 m (intervals; see chapter 20 **Run** 3 miles easy
Tuesday	**Bike** 105 minutes hard + **Strength**	**Bike** 110 minutes hard + **Strength**	**Bike** 115 minutes hard	**Bike** 105 minutes hard + **Strength**
Wednesday	**Run** 6K tempo run	**Run** 7K tempo run	**Run** 7K tempo run, **Strength**	**Run** 5K tempo run
Thursday	**Swim** 2,900 m (speed work) open-water swim Strength	**Swim** 3,000 m (speed work) open-water swim Strength	**Swim** 3,100 m (speed work) open-water swim Run 6 miles	**Swim** 2,900 m (speed work) open-water swim
Friday	Rest or Active Recovery	Rest or Active Recovery	Rest or Active Recovery	Rest or Active Recovery
Saturday	**Bike** 190 minutes	**Bike** 200 minutes	**Bike** 210 minutes	**Bike** 190 minutes
Sunday	**Run** 4 miles easy	**Brick:** **Bike** 110 minutes + **Run** 2 miles	**Brick:** **Bike** 115 minutes + **Run** 3 miles	**Brick Bike** 105 minutes + **Run** 1 mile

Weeks 18–20: Taper and Race Preparation

	Week 18	Week 19 (Taper week)	Week 20 (Race week)
Monday	**Swim** 3,300 m (speed work) open-water swim **Run** 4 miles moderate pace	**Swim** 2,000 m (easy pace) open-water swim	Rest
Tuesday	**Bike** 125 minutes moderate + **Strength**	**Bike** 90 minutes easy pace	**Bike** 60 minutes easy

	Week 18	Week 19 (Taper week)	Week 20 (Race week)
Wednesday	**Run** 6 miles easy pace	**Run** 5K easy pace	**Run** 30 minutes easy
Thursday	**Swim** 3,300 m (speed work) open-water swim	**Swim** open-water swim 1,500 m	Open-water **swim** – 1,500 m
Friday	Rest or Active Recovery	Rest or active recovery	Off
Saturday	**Bike** 160 minutes	**Bike** 1 hour	Quick 20-minute open-water **swim**, 30-minute bike, 10-minute **run**
Sunday	**Brick**: **Bike** 125 minutes + **Run** 3 miles	**Run** 1 hour	Race day!

20-week Olympic Training Plan for a New Triathlete

The following is a 20-week triathlon training plan for beginners wanting to complete an Olympic triathlon. An Olympic triathlon typically consists of a 1.5K swim, a 40K bike ride, and a 10K run.

If the swim is not specified, it's a freestyle swim. Everything is in meters, so if you are at a "yard" pool, do the same workout. Codes are as follows:

- WU: means warm-up
- DS: means drill set
- MS: means main set
- CD: cool-down
- Strength: strength training
- Swim: this means freestyle swim

Take a break when you need it. Try to stick with a 30-second rest. Also, I included two strength workouts. They should be approximately 30 minutes.

Finally, you can move the schedule around. If you have something on a particular day, change it. This program serves as a guideline for you to follow, but it is subject to change.

Weeks 1-4: Base Building Phase

	Week 1	Week 2	Week 3	Week 4 (Recovery)
Monday	**Swim** 300 m (rest as needed) **WU:** 50 m **Kick:** 50 m with fins and paddles Pull 50 m with pull buoy and paddles Kick 50 m Swim 50 m **CD:** 50 m pull buoy and paddles	**Swim** 400 m (rest as needed) **WU:** 100 m straight, nice and easy **DS:** 2 × 25 drill/25 swim, your choice **MS:** 50 m rest for 20 seconds; 50 free, rest 20 seconds; 50 free, rest 20 seconds **CD:** 2 × 25 easy Strength	**Swim** 500 m **WU:** 100 m **DS:** pick 4 × 25 drill/25 swim **MS:** 100 m straight with or without fins; 50 m paddles and buoy **CD:** 50 m easy swim After swim run: 2 miles at a tempo pace; see chapter 30	**Swim** 300 m (rest as needed) **WU:** 50 m **Kick:** 50 m with fins and paddles Pull 50 m with pull buoy and paddles Kick 50 m Swim 50 m **CD:** 50 m pull buoy and paddles
Tuesday	**Bike** 30 minutes easy pace, **Strength**	**Bike** 35 minutes easy pace	**Bike** 40 minutes easy pace, **Strength**	**Bike** 30 minutes easy pace
Wednesday	**Run** 2 miles easy pace	**Run** 2.5 miles easy pace, **Strength**	**Run** 2.5 miles easy pace	**Run** 2 miles easy pace
Thursday	**Swim** 300 m (rest as needed) **WU:** 100 m **DS:** 2 × 25 drill/25 swim **CD:** 100 m swim Strength	**Swim** 400 m any stroke for 4 × 100 m rest 1 minute in between	**Swim** 500 m (rest as needed) **WU:** 50 m **MS:** 200 m no stopping; 50 m swim; 100 m swim **CD:** 100 m backstroke **Strength**	**Swim** 300 m (rest as needed) **WU:** 100 m **DS:** 2 × 25 drill/25 swim **CD:** 100 m swim
Friday	Rest or Active Recovery	Rest or Active Recovery	Rest or Active Recovery	Rest or Active Recovery
Saturday	**Bike** 45 minutes easy pace	**Bike** 50 minutes easy pace	**Bike** 55 minutes easy pace	**Bike** 45 minutes easy pace
Sunday	**Brick**: **Bike** 30 minutes + **Run** 0.5 mile	**Brick Bike** 35 minutes + **Run** 1 mile	**Brick:** **Bike** 40 minutes + **Run** 1 miles	**Brick:** **Bike** 30 minutes + **Run** .5 mile

Weeks 5-8: Endurance Phase

	Week 5	Week 6	Week 7 (Recovery)	Week 8
Monday	**Swim** 750 m (rest as needed) **WU:** 100 m straight, 30 sec rest **DS:** 4 × 25 drill/25 swim **MS:** 100 m straight swim; 100 m swim; 50 m Fast/50 m slow **CD:** 150 m easy	**Swim** 800 m **WU:** 200 m straight, nice and easy **DS:** 100 m in drills, choice (see section on drills) **MS:** 100 m rest for 20 seconds; 50 m free, rest 20 seconds; 100 m free, rest 20 seconds; 50 m Fast **CD:** 200 m easy **Run** 3 miles	**Swim** 750 m (rest as needed) **WU:** 100 straight, 30 sec rest **DS:** 4 × 25 drill/25 swim **MS:** 100 m straight swim; 100 m swim; 50 m Fast/50 m slow **CD:** 150 m easy	**Swim** 1,000 m (rest as needed) **WU:** 200 m easy MS: 300 m moderate swim; 200 m moderate; 100 m moderate **CD:** 200 m easy **Run** after swim 3 miles
Tuesday	**Bike** 50 minutes moderate pace, **Strength**	**Bike** 55 minutes moderate pace, **Strength**	**Bike** 50 minutes moderate pace, **Strength**	**Bike** 65 minutes moderate pace, **Strength**
Wednesday	**Run** 4 miles easy pace	**Run** 3.5 miles easy pace	**Run** 3 miles easy pace	**Run** 5.5 miles easy pace
Thursday	**Swim** 750 m (rest as needed) open-water swim today **Run** after swim: 2 miles	**Swim** 800 m open-water swim **Strength**	**Swim** 750 m (rest as needed) open-water swim today **Run** after swim 3 miles	**Swim** 1,000 m (rest as needed) open-water swim **Strength**
Friday	Rest or Active Recovery	Rest or Active Recovery	Rest or Active Recovery	Rest or Active Recovery
Saturday	**Bike** 65 minutes moderate pace, **Strength**	**Bike** 70 minutes moderate pace	**Bike** 65 minutes moderate pace, **Strength**	**Bike** 80 minutes moderate pace
Sunday	**Brick:** **Bike** 50 minutes + **Run** 1 miles	**Brick:** **Bike** 55 minutes + **Run** 1.5 miles	**Brick:** **Bike** 50 minutes + **Run** 1 mile	**Brick:** **Bike** 65 minutes + **Run** 1.5 miles

Weeks 9–12: Build Phase

	Week 9	Week 10	Week 11 (Recovery)	Week 12
Monday	**Swim** 1,100 m (rest as needed) open-water swim **Run** 4 miles	**Swim** 1,200 m (rest as needed) open-water swim **Run** 4 miles moderate	**Swim** 1,000 m (rest as needed) **WU:** 200 m **MS:** 300 m moderate; 200 m moderate;100 m moderate **CD:** 200 m easy Run after swim 2 miles	**Swim** 1,400 m (rest as needed) **WU:** 300 m **MS:** 400 m with fins and paddles; 300 m with paddles and buoy; 200 m with kickboard and fins; 100 m swim **CD:** 100 m easy **Run** 4 miles tempo pace **Strength**
Tuesday	**Bike** 70 minutes moderate pace **Strength**	**Bike** 75 minutes moderate pace **Strength**	**Bike** 65 minutes moderate pace	**Bike** 85 minutes moderate pace
Wednesday	**Run** 6 miles easy pace	**Run** 6.5 miles easy pace	**Run** 3.5 miles easy pace	**Run** 5 miles easy pace, **Strength**
Thursday	**Swim** 1,100 m (rest as needed) open-water swim **Strength**	**Swim** 1,200 m (rest as needed) open-water swim **Strength**	**Swim** 1,000 m (rest as needed) open-water swim	**Swim** 1,400 m (rest as needed) open-water swim
Friday	Rest or Active Recovery	Rest or Active Recovery	Rest or Active Recovery	Rest or Active Recovery
Saturday	**Bike** 85 minutes moderate pace	**Bike** 90 minutes moderate pace	**Bike** 80 minutes moderate pace	**Bike** 100 minutes moderate pace
Sunday	**Brick:** **Bike** 70 minutes + **Run** 2 miles	**Brick:** **Bike** 75 minutes + **Run** 2 miles	**Brick:** **Bike** 65 minutes + **Run** 1.5 miles	**Brick**: **Bike** 85 minutes + **Run** 2 miles

Weeks 13–16: Peak Volume Phase

	Week 13	Week 14	Week 15 (Recovery)	Week 16
Monday	**Swim** 1,500 m (intervals) open-water swim; see chapter 20 **Strength**	**Swim** 1,600 m (intervals) open-water swim **Run** 4 miles around a track, moderate-to-easy pace	**Swim** 1,400 m (rest as needed) **WU:** 300 m easy **MS:** 400 m with fins and paddles; 300 m with paddles and buoy; 200 m with kickboard and fins; 100 m swim **CD:** 100 Easy **Run** 3 miles tempo pace	**Swim** 1,800 m (intervals) open-water swim **Strength**
Tuesday	**Bike** 90 minutes moderate/hard pace	**Bike** 95 minutes moderate/hard pace **Strength**	**Bike** 85 minutes moderate pace	**Bike** 105 minutes moderate/hard pace
Wednesday	**Run** 6 miles tempo run, **Strength**	**Run** 6.5 miles tempo run	**Run** 4 miles easy pace	**Run** 7 miles tempo run
Thursday	**Swim** 1,500 m (endurance) open-water swim (see how far you can go without stopping) **Run** 4 miles easy	**Swim** 1,600 m (endurance) open-water swim **Strength**	**Swim** 1,400 m open-water swim	**Swim** 1,800 m (endurance) open-water swim **Strength**
Friday	Rest or Active Recovery	Rest or Active Recovery	Rest or Active Recovery	Rest or Active Recovery
Saturday	**Bike** 105 minutes moderate/hard pace	**Bike** 110 minutes moderate/hard pace	**Bike** 100 minutes moderate pace	**Bike** 120 minutes moderate/hard pace
Sunday	**Brick Bike** 90 minutes + **Run** 2 miles	**Brick:** **Bike** 95 minutes + **Run** 2 miles	**Brick:** **Bike** 85 minutes + **Run** 1 mile	**Brick:** **Bike** 105 minutes + **Run** 2 miles

Weeks 17–20: Taper and Race Preparation

	Week 17	Week 18	Week 19 (Taper)	Week 20 (Race week)
Monday	**Swim** 2,000 m (speed work) **WU:** 300 m swim **MS:** 100 m Fast × 6 with 30 seconds rest in between each set; 50 m slow/50 m Fast + 100 m Fast × 5 **CD:** 100 slow **Strength**	**Swim** 2,000 m (speed work) open-water swim **Run** 3 miles moderate	**Swim** 1,500 m easy open-water swim	Off
Tuesday	**Bike** 90 minutes moderate pace	**Bike** 85 minutes moderate pace	Off	**Swim** 1,000 m easy open water
Wednesday	**Run** 7 miles easy pace **Strength**	**Run** 6 miles easy pace, **Strength**	**Run** 5 miles easy	**Run** 3 miles
Thursday	**Swim** 2,000 m (speed work) open-water swim	**Swim** 2,000 m (speed work) open-water swim **Strength**	**Swim** 1,500 m easy open water	Off
Friday	Rest or Active Recovery	Rest or Active Recovery	Rest	Quick tri 20-minute open-water swim, 30-minute bike, 10-minute run
Saturday	**Bike** 100 minutes moderate pace	**Bike** 90 minutes moderate pace	**Bike** 60 minutes	Off
Sunday	**Brick**: **Bike** 90 minutes + **Run** 2 miles	**Brick**: **Bike** 85 minutes + **Run** 3 miles	**Run** 60 minutes	Race day!

20-Week Olympic Training Plan for an Experienced Triathlete

Here is a detailed 20-week training plan for an experienced triathlete aiming to podium in their next Olympic triathlon. This plan builds endurance, speed, and strength while incorporating specific race simulation workouts. Remember to review the book for other workouts if needed including bike and run workouts. Additionally, include 2 days of strength training, with a minimum of 30 minutes each day. Your choice of day. See book for detailed workouts.

If the swim is not specified, it's a freestyle swim. Everything is in meters (m), so if you are at a "yard" pool, do the same workout. Codes are as follows:

- WU: means warm-up
- DS: means drill set
- MS: means main set
- CD: cool-down
- Strength: strength training
- Swim: This means freestyle swim

Take a break when you need it. Try to stick with a 30-second rest. Also, I included two strength workouts. They should be approximately 30 minutes.

Finally, you can move the schedule around. If you have something on a particular day, change it. This program serves as a guideline for you to follow, but it is subject to change.

Weeks 1-4: Base Building Phase

	Week 1	Week 2	Week 3	Week 4 (Recovery)
Monday	**Swim** 1,500 m (technique focus) **WU:** 400 m easy swim **DS:** 8 × 25 drill/25 swim, rest 30 seconds in between **MS:** 400 m swim; 100 m Fast **CD:** 200 m easy Run after swim 2 miles	**Swim** 1,600 m (technique focus) **WU:** 300 m **DS:** 4 × 25 kick with kickboard and fins; 4 × 25 drill of choice/25 swim **MS:** 100 m × 8 easy **CD:** 200 m slow Run 2 miles	**Swim** 1,700 m (technique focus) **WU:** 300 m **DS:** 4 × choice 25 drill/25 swim **MS:** 400 m swim with fins and paddles; 300 m swim with fins; 200 m swim with pull buoy and paddles; 100 m kick board with fins; 50 m Swim Fast; 50 swim slow **CD:** 100 m choice	**Swim** 1,500 m (technique focus) **WU:** 300 m easy **DS:** 8 × 25 drill/25 swim, rest 30 seconds in between **MS:** 400 m swim; 100 m Fast **CD:** 300 m easy **Run** after swim 2 miles
Tuesday	**Bike** 60 minutes easy	**Bike** 65 minutes easy **Strength**	**Bike** 70 minutes easy **Strength**	**Bike** 60 minutes easy
Wednesday	**Run** 3 mile easy pace	**Run** 4K easy pace	**Run** 5K easy pace	**Run** 5K easy pace
Thursday	**Swim** 1,500 m (endurance) open-water swim (let's see what you got!)	**Swim** 1,600 m (endurance) open-water swim **Strength**	**Swim** 1,700 m (endurance) open-water swim **Strength**	**Swim** 1,500 m (endurance) open-water swim (let's see what you got!)
Friday	Rest or Active Recovery	Rest or Active Recovery	Rest or Active Recovery	Rest or Active Recovery
Saturday	**Bike** 90 minutes easy	**Bike** 95 minutes easy	**Bike** 100 minutes easy	**Bike** 90 minutes easy
Sunday	**Brick:** **Bike** 60 minutes + **Run** 1 mile	**Brick:** **Bike** 65 minutes + **Run** 1 mile	**Brick:** **Bike** 70 minutes + **Run** 1 mile	**Run** 60 minutes

Weeks 5–8: Build Phase

	Week 5	Week 6	Week 7	Week 8
Monday	**Swim** 2,000 m (intervals) open-water swim **Run** 4 miles moderate	**Swim** 2,100 m (intervals) open-water swim **Run** 3 miles	**Swim** 2,200 m (intervals) open-water swim **Run** 4 miles	**Swim** 2,000 m (intervals) open-water swim **Run** 3 miles moderate
Tuesday	**Bike** 80 minutes moderate **Strength**	**Bike** 85 minutes moderate **Strength**	**Bike** 90 minutes moderate **Strength**	**Bike** 80 minutes moderate **Strength**
Wednesday	**Run** 4 miles moderate pace	**Run** 5 miles moderate pace	**Run** 6 miles moderate pace	**Run** 3 miles moderate pace
Thursday	**Swim** 2,000 m (endurance) open-water swim	**Swim** 2,100 m (endurance) Try to do this one in the pool focusing on stroke and endurance **WU:** 400 m **MS:** 1,500 m straight **CD:** 200 m Strength	**Swim** 2,200 m (endurance) open-water swim **Strength**	**Swim** 2,000 m (endurance) open-water swim **Strength**
Friday	Rest or Active Recovery	Rest or Active Recovery	Rest or Active Recovery	Rest or Active Recovery
Saturday	**Bike** 110 minutes moderate **Strength**	**Bike** 115 minutes moderate	**Bike** 120 minutes moderate	**Bike** 110 minutes moderate
Sunday	**Brick:** **Bike** 80 minutes + **Run** 2 miles	**Brick:** **Bike** 85 minutes + **Run** 2 miles	**Brick:** **Bike** 90 minutes + **Run** 1.5 miles	**Brick:** **Bike** 80 minutes + **Run** 1 mile

Weeks 9–12: Peak Volume Phase

	Week 9	Week 10	Week 11	Week 12 (Recovery)
Monday	**Swim** 2,400 m (speed work) open-water swim (See chapter 20) **Run** 5 miles	**Swim** 2,500 m (speed work) open-water swim; see chapter 20 **Run** 6 miles easy	**Swim** 2,600 m (speed work) open-water swim **Run** 6 miles easy	**Swim** 2,400 m (speed work) open-water swim; see chapter 20 **Run** 3 miles
Tuesday	**Bike** 100 minutes moderate/ Hard **Strength**	**Bike** 105 minutes moderate/ hard	**Bike** 110 minutes moderate/ hard Strength	**Bike** 100 minutes moderate/hard
Wednesday	**Run** 7 miles tempo run	**Run** 8 miles tempo run	**Run** 9 miles tempo run	**Run** 4 miles tempo run
Thursday	**Swim** 2,400 m (endurance) open-water swim try to go as long as you can without stopping **Strength**	**Swim** 2,500 m (endurance) open-water swim	**Swim** 2,600 m (endurance) open-water swim **Strength**	**Swim** 2,400 m (endurance) open-water swim try to go as long as you can without stopping
Friday	Rest or Active Recovery	Rest or Active Recovery	Rest or Active Recovery	Rest or Active Recovery
Saturday	**Bike** 130 minutes moderate/hard	**Bike** 135 minutes moderate/hard	**Bike 140** minutes moderate/hard	**Bike** 130 minutes moderate/hard
Sunday	**Brick**: **Bike** 100 minutes + **Run** 2 miles	**Brick:** **Bike** 105 minutes + **Run** 2 miles	**Brick:** **Bike** 110 minutes + **Run** 1.5 miles	**Brick:** **Bike** 100 minutes + **Run** 1 mile

Weeks 13-16: Speed and Intensity Phase

	Week 13	Week 14	Week 15	Week 16 (Recovery)
Monday	**Swim** 2,800 m (intervals) open-water swim	**Swim** 2,900 m (intervals) open-water swim Run 3 miles easy	**Swim** 3,000 m (intervals) open-water swim Run 3 miles	**Swim** 2,500 m (intervals) open-water swim
Tuesday	**Bike** 120 minutes hard **Strength**	**Bike** 125 minutes hard **Strength**	**Bike** 130 minutes hard **Strength**	**Bike** 120 **minutes** hard
Wednesday	**Run** 5 miles speed intervals	**Run** 7 miles speed intervals	**Run** 6 miles speed intervals	**Run** 6 miles speed intervals
Thursday	**Swim** 2,800 m (speed work) **WU:** 200 m choice; 100 m Kick **MS:** 450 m choice; 50 m choice; 200 m × 5 Fast with 30 second rest; 400 m choice; 100 m choice; 200 m choice **CD:** 300 m easy Strength	**Swim** 2,900 m (speed work) open-water swim **Strength**	**Swim** 3,000 m (speed work) open-water swim **Strength**	**Swim** 2,800 m (speed work) **WU:** 200 m choice; 100 Kick **MS:** 450 m choice; 50 m choice; 200 m × 5 Fast with 30 second rest; 400 m choice; 100 m choice; 200 m choice **CD:** 300 m easy
Friday	Rest or Active Recovery	Rest or Active Recovery	Rest or Active Recovery	Rest or Active Recovery
Saturday	**Bike** 150 minutes hard	**Bike** 155 minutes hard	**Bike** 160 minutes hard	**Bike** 150 minutes hard
Sunday	**Brick:** **Bike** 120 minutes + **Run** 2 miles	**Brick:** **Bike** 125 minutes + **Run** 1 mile	**Brick**: **Bike** 130 minutes + **Run** 1 mile	**Brick: Bike** 120 minutes + **Run** 2 miles

Weeks 17–20: Taper and Race Preparation

	Week 17	Week 18	Week 19 (Taper)	Week 20 (Race week)
Monday	**Swim** 3,200 m (speed work) open-water swim	**Swim** 3,300 m (speed work) open-water swim Strength	**Swim** 2,000 m (easy pace) open-water swim	**Swim** 1,500 m open water
Tuesday	**Bike** 120 minutes moderate **Strength**	**Bike** 115 minutes moderate	**Bike** 90 minutes easy pace	**Bike** 60-minutes
Wednesday	**Run** 7 miles easy pace	**Run** 8-mile easy pace	**Run** 6 miles easy pace	**Run** 3-miles shake-out run
Thursday	**Swim** 3,200 m (speed work) open-water swim **Strength**	**Swim** 3,300 m (speed work) open-water swim **Strength**	**Swim** 1,000 m open-water swim	Off
Friday	Rest or Active Recovery	Rest or Active Recovery	Rest	Swim open water for 20 minutes, bike for 30 minutes, run for 10 minutes as one event
Saturday	**Bike** 130 minutes moderate	**Bike** 120 minutes moderate	**Bike** 60 minutes	Off
Sunday	**Brick:** **Bike** 120 minutes + **Run** 2 miles	**Brick:** **Bike** 115 minutes + **Run** 2 miles	**Run** 60 minutes Easy	Race day!

SUGGESTED READING

Throughout my decade-long journey as a triathlete, I've read numerous books. While some have been truly beneficial, others have not. Here, I share a curated list of recommended books alongside *Unlocking the Triathlon.*

Swimming

Hutchinson, Alexander "The Swim Prescription: How Swimming Can Improve Your Mood, Restore Health, Increase Physical Fitness and Revitalize Your Life." Hatherleigh Press, 2022

Lucero, Blythe "Swim Fast: 100 Workouts to Improve Your Swim Technique." Meyer & Meyer Sport, 2023

Tsui, Bonnie "Why We Swim." Algonquin Books, 2020

Cycling

Bortman, Tori "The Bicycling Big Book of Cycling for Beginners: Everything a new cyclist needs to know to gear up and start riding." Rodale Books; Illustrated edition, 2014

Running

Galloway, Jeff "Run Walk Run Method." Meyer & Meyer Sport; 3rd edition, 2024

Galloway, Jeff "Galloway's Half Marathon Training: Use the Run Walk Run Method to Finish Every Race Strong." Meyer & Meyer Sport; 5th edition, 2021

McDougall, Christopher "Born to Run: A Hidden Tribe, Superathletes, and the Greatest Race the World Has Never Seen." Knopf, 1st edition, 2009

Triathlon

Atwood, Meredith "Triathlon for the Every Woman: You Can Be a Triathlete. Yes. You." Da Capo Lifelong Books, 2019

Dixon, Matt "The Well-Built Triathlete: Turning Potential into Performance." VeloPress Books, 2014

Ford, Fiona "Back on Track: How I Recovered from a Near-Fatal Accident and Got Back on My Feet." Meyer & Meyer Sport, 2020

Friel, Joe "Fast After 50: How to Race Strong for the Rest of Your Life." VeloPress Books, 2015

Topper, Hilary "From Couch Potato to Endurance Athlete: A Portrait of a Non-Athletic Triathlete." Meyer & Meyer Sport, 2022

Fitzgerald, Matt and Warden, David "80/20 Triathlon: Discover the Breakthrough Elite-Training Formula for Ultimate Fitness and Performance at All Levels." Da Capo Lifelong Books, 2018

Jorgensen, Gwen, Jorgensen, Nancy, and Jorgensen, Elizabeth "Gwen Jorgensen: USA's First Olympic Gold Medal Triathlete." Meyer & Meyer Sport, 2022

Lacke, Susan "Life's Too Short to Go So F*cking Slow: Lessons from an Epic Friendship That Went the Distance." VeloPress Books, 2017

Moss, Julie and Yehling, Robert "Crawl of Fame: Julie Moss and the Fifteen Feet that Created an Ironman Triathlon Legend." Pegasus Books, 2018

Wellington, Chrissie "A Life Without Limits: A World Champion's Journey." Center Street; 1st edition, 2012

Strength Training

Hagerman, Patrick "Strength Training for Triathletes: The Complete Program to Build Triathlon Power, Speed, and Muscular Endurance." VeloPress Books, 2024

Nutrition

Sims, Stacy T "ROAR, Revised Edition: Match Your Food and Fitness to Your Unique Female Physiology for Optimum Performance, Great Health, and a Strong Body for Life." Rodale Books, 2024

ABOUT THE AUTHOR

Hilary J. M. Topper, MPA, is a triathlete. She started training for triathlons in 2014 and has completed numerous triathlons and running races. Hilary is a USAT Coach, USMS Swim Coach Level 3, a WOWSA Open Water Swim Coach, and an RRCA Run Coach. She coaches individual athletes and has a swimming and running group.

Hilary is a public relations practitioner and started her business, HJMT PR, in 1992. She helped companies with publicity and social media marketing.

Today, she has a media company, HJMT Media Co., LLC, where she writes two blogs–a NY Lifestyle Blog, hilarytopper.com, and *atriathletesdiary.com*. She also started a podcast, Hilary Topper on Air in 2011.

Hilary is the author of three books, including *Everything You Ever Wanted to Know About Social Media*, published in 2009. It was the first social media book of its kind. In 2019, she wrote *Branding in a Digital World,* specifically for her class at Hofstra University. She recently revised it in 2023. Students use the book as a textbook. It was also written for new business owners to learn to brand and build their businesses.

Her most recent book, *From Couch Potato to Endurance Athlete: A Portrait of a Non-Athletic Triathlete*, is a memoir that takes the reader on a 10-year journey from the author's early days when she first started running. The book is available from Meyer & Meyer Sport through their affiliate, Cardinal Press.

Hilary lives in Merrick, New York, with her husband. They have two adult children, one married with a baby and a dog.

St. Croix's 2018
Triathlon
VI TRI
Real Nice
WeRTriathletes
515

MORE FROM HILARY TOPPER!

$18.95 US

ISBN: 978-1-78255-240-6

Hilary Topper

GET INSPIRED TO GET ACTIVE!

For those who have ever thought they were too old or too unfit to finish a triathlon, *From Couch Potato to Endurance Athlete* will prove that it is never too late to compete! Hilary`s story will move, motivate, and inspire. You will laugh and cry as you follow her on her journey. Even if you don`t start out as an endurance athlete, after reading this book, you will walk away feeling that no matter what happens, you can cross the finish line, too.

MEYER & MEYER Sport
Von-Coels-Str. 390
52080 Aachen
Germany

Phone +49 02 41 - 9 58 10 - 13
Fax +49 02 41 - 9 58 10 - 10
E-Mail sales@m-m-sports.com
Website www.m-m-sports.com

MEYER
& MEYER
SPORT

Credits

Cover and interior design:	Anja Elsen
Layout:	DiTech Publishing Servies, www.ditechpubs.com
Cover photo:	Courtesy of the author; the publisher controls right to use of images
Interior photos:	Courtesy of the author, unless otherwise noted; all sidebar photos are used with permission; the publisher controls right to use of images
Managing editor:	Elizabeth Evans
Copy editor:	Sarah Tomblin, www.sarahtomblinediting.com